PASSION IN
Poetry:
Whispers from
the Soul

PASSION IN Poetry:
Whispers from the Soul

Nandita 'Manan' Yata

PARTRIDGE

To order additional copies of this book, contact
Partridge India
000 800 10062 62
orders.india@partridgepublishing.com

www.partridgepublishing.com/india

CONTENTS

LIFE

LONGINGS

LOVE

To

Ama, whose unwritten poetry runs deep in my veins

and

Amanya, the most beautiful poem I have created

Acknowledgements

No artist is complete without a Muse. No art can be started and perfected without inspiration. Many people have helped me in ways known and unknown in bringing my first book on poetry to fruition. From the bottom of my grateful heart, I would like to begin by thanking my Muse of Poetry for making a poet out of me. My sweetest love and priceless gift Amanya, my immediate family (Ama, Ajoy, Namrata, Prashant) whose love is the greatest blessing in my life. And my entire family of aunts, uncles, cousins, nephews, and nieces who make up my world of love and trust.

Bestie Rhema Sereng, soul sis Jashoda Chettri, Madhushree Chatterjee, Swati Pal, Sangeeta Aggarwal for being with me through thick and thin. Aashish Gurung, Anuja Tyagi, Pema (Pem Quirk), Naresh Singh, Devashish Sriwal, Raj Chettri, Neelam Gurung, Zubair Agloria, Selina Lepcha, En Christina for being some of my earliest readers and all my Dead Poets Society members for all encouragement.

Manjit Saikia has been an important part in this soul searching journey, introducing me to blog world and thereby opening up a bright new window to a world I have always belonged to but was unable to find my way. I will always remain grateful to you for that. Thank you also for letting me use your breathtaking images.

Wonderful fellow poets and kindred souls who mean a lot to me: Dave Meriwether, Jonathan Noble, Joseph Parent, Kyrsia Korsak, Priyanka Ruth, Rosemarie Gonzales, Tony Single for all the love you have for me which you show everyday. You are my Serenading Seven! Special shout-out to Jonathan and Tony.

Friends Andrew, Antony, Aruna, Charlie, Dori, Kunal, Matthew, Melinda, Ryan from the blog world who have now left their marks some way or the other in my heart. I'm in your corner and you are all in my circle.

Many thanks to all my loving readers on WordPress.

FT Ledrew, my partnering poet, my Lord of the Pen in my writing world. Thank you Thomas, for taking the pain (with a smile) of reading everything I have ever written (over 450 poems and prose pieces and still counting) to help me come up with my manuscript and for proofreading, editing and for simply being what you are to me. I couldn't have asked for a better poet to do the honours. Thank you for adorning my soul work with bits of your own in the form of your beautiful words and fabulous images. You are the dawn to my dusk, the light to my dark, the stanzas to my lines and all the sacred interludes. Beginning with the preordained 'loves typos', every single 'phase' has been a journey of 'divine friendship' where the 'sands of time' saw us 'borrowing dawn', enthralled by our 'chat with raindrops' while the jealous sky watched the artist being 'caught out loud' in his praise of the muse.

Foreword

"I decided that it was not wisdom that enabled poets to write their poetry, but a kind of instinct or inspiration, such as you find in seers and prophets who deliver all their sublime messages without knowing in the least what they mean."

~ Socrates

When Nandita Yata asked if I would write a foreword to her debut book of poetry, ***Passion in Poetry: Whispers from the Soul***, I was humbled because I had not known her long, even though I had read everything she had written and posted to her blog, **Manan Unleashed** (www.mananunleashed. wordpress.com). Then, she quickly reminded me that I understood her writing as well as she understood herself. So, I eagerly accepted the challenge and armed with her manuscript, I set to penning this introduction to Nandita and her work.

A native of India, Nandita Yata is a prolific writer, often penning many poems a day. She is easily inspired by people and place, and is inspirational at the same time. Paying attention to her Muse(s), she is adept at capturing life, passion, pain and love through a myriad of poetic forms, including etheree, lanturne, lune, senryu, sonnet. For Nandita, writing poetry is as important as oxygen. In fact, she will tell you that the day she stops writing poetry is the day she no longer breathes. In "I Rain, I Write", Nandita explains:

> I wrote.
> Like that was the only thing I knew.
> Like that was the only way I could save myself.
>
> I write.
> Because, I will die if I don't!

Nandita's words remind me of Shelley who wrote:

> Poetry is a sword of lightning, ever unsheathed, which consumes the scabbard that would contain it.

This may appear to be extreme hyperbole, however, it speaks to importance of poetry in her daily life. And she is not alone in her connection to poetry. Pablo Neruda, in "Poesia" describes the pull of poetry in his life:

> And it was at that age ... Poetry He came
> looking for me. I do not know, do not know
> where
> it came from…
> I do not know how or when…
> it touched me.

Neruda goes on to explain in "Poet's Obligation":

...And I shall broadcast, saying nothing,
the starry echoes of the wave,
a breaking up of foam and quicksand,
a rustling of salt withdrawing,
the grey cry of the sea-birds on the coast.
So, through me, freedom and the sea
will make their answer to the shuttered heart.

With the poetic understanding and same sense of obligation as Neruda, Nandita has a sound grasp of her connection to the world around her. She writes what she lives and she lives what she writes. For her, the relationship with poetry is symbiotic and like Rumi she is "neither of the East nor of the West, no boundaries exist within my breast", thus freeing her to be herself.

Just as impressive as her grasp of life, passion, pain and love, is Nandita's ability to share such understanding through fresh, uncomplicated poetry. Her lines are filled with simple language that is easily understood, yet, for those looking for more depth she provides a world in which mysteries abound, often hiding deeper messages within the stanzas. At the same time, Nandita is able to apply both literal and figurative language to create the perfect balance in many of her works as can be seen in "Poetry Everywhere".

Poetry is love and love is poetry
In between you see the beauty
All the manifestations in all its glory
No matter the language – wordless or flowery

There's a line in every word, a verse in every line
A story hidden to be unwrapped in its layer
So open the eyes of the mind divine
When you do, you'll see there's poetry everywhere

There is also something else alluring about Nandita's poetic prowess and that is her ability to share her pen with other writers. A couple of months ago, I had the opportunity to write a number of collaborations with her (all have been included in this book) and she is, by far, the most versatile writer I know and so adaptable to the writing styles of others, that any collaboration she pens is seamless. This is a testament to the deep connection she has with other like-minded poets. In fact, as I type this, her time is being requested by other poets at such a rate, that she has had to open a second blog for sharing these duets. You can find all her collaborations at **Manan Chained** (mananchained. wordpress.com).

Empathetic, sensitive, intelligent, keenly observant, reflective, creative and a professed lover of sunsets, Nandita Yata is a universal poetess for the ages. When the soul speaks, Nandita listens, ponders and then writes the most beautiful poetry. ***Passion in Poetry: Whispers from the Soul***, is a testament to the poetry she eats, sleeps and breathes and to her humanity. Ladies and Gentlemen, it is my honour and privilege to present to you, Nandita Yata.

FT Ledrew
Herring Neck, Newfoundland
May 4, 2016

FT Ledrew is a musician and writer living on the Northeast coast of Newfoundland, Canada. His blog, Hook, Line and Inkwell, can be found at hooklineandinkwell.wordpress.com.

Not the ones speaking the same language but the ones sharing the same feeling understand each other.

~ Rumi

LIFE

A Karmic Conversation

I chose love but love didn't choose me
I broke several hearts to mend one heart
I fell insanely in love with one
Too sane and rational for the reckless me!

Today Karma came to me in my dream
I had been sleeping fitfully
I was screaming but my voice was drowning
In the echoes of your goodbyes

I was reduced to a mere granule of sand
By the shadows of your dark light
Karma smirked at me
But there was sadness too in his voice

When he said,
Silly girl, why do you weep?
Don't you know
You only get what you give!

And then I heard it
All those maddening screams
They all cursed me save one
That said, you are the chosen one

"You were destined"
Karma spoke again, "To show one
How to love
Your work is now done".

A Life without Dreams

Close my eyes
Darkness outside
Cross my heart
Nothingness inside

I look above
The sky has fallen
I stand still
Shaky and trembling

My eyes downcast
An unending abyss
Hope is buried
Down below

Love is a dream
Life goes on
I live still
A life without dreams

Bleed Away the Blue

Bleed away the blue like I always do
Get that pain out, you know that it is true
Words and lines can so help you make it through
Release, get soaked in your blood, feel anew

Bleed away the blue, I know you want to
Get your act together with no ado
Our lot is blessed with abnormal tear ducts
We feel the pain on reading your poem's crux

Bleed away the blue, don't keep it hidden
Give it shape, A to Z, feelings laden
There is so much you hold, let it release
Feel your heart swell, rise and brim, feel it please

Bleed away the blue, that's what you do best
Poetry has blessed you, don't put it to rest

Blue Bird

Voices outside tell me to let go
Of what I'm clutching too hard
I dismiss them all, look the other way
I tell them I like to be charred

All day long I hear voices
Coaxing me to abide
This is not doing you any good
They rebuke they mock they chide

A voice within whispers to me
Your strength is misunderstood
Believe in what you love and hold
Let time decide what is bad or good

All day long I hear this voice
Fly free soar high in the blue skies
As long as you are trying I'm staying
It cajoles it soothes it pacifies

Fly away my blue bird
I mustn't keep you any longer
I have shushed you too long
You were meant to be free and stronger

Break Free, Fall Freer

You have held yourself back too long
Tried to tell yourself you are strong
All the while harbouring a fragile heart
Just too scared to make a start

It's alright to fear a little
When you've been made brittle
By what you thought was your strength
Sapping you out of your energy at length

Don't let experiences make you bitter
Make them make you better
If you truly want NOW to matter
You need to be untie the tether

Free yourself from your own prison
Cage the demon don't give it a reason
To stop you from achieving
That what your heart is truly pining
But what your mind is so denying

Just get free falling
Never mind the stumbling

Cosmic Brew

Souls meet in ways mysterious
Unfathomable to those who are not serious
About the unravelling of the unknown
Or the seed that has already been sown

As Coelho puts it, the universe conspires
To bring to the heart that earnestly desires
Souls have a way of finding and being found
Soulmates, separated though at times, are always around

The seed is long sown, no one knows how and when
The cosmos waters the plant every now and then
Why does it take aeons to be found is a question I ask
Getting the answer to this is a daunting task

Not all mysteries are meant to be solved
We are on a journey, to be found and be loved
Some are found, others carry on and wander
Not all soulmates are meant to be together

But a tryst in some lifetime or the other, no heaven no hell
Short long eternal transient no one can tell
All the unfolding of the cosmic conspiracy,
so immaculately true
Only if you believe, you can delve into the depths of the
cosmic brew

Crossover*

It's black all around
I know I'm nearing home, for
I see the white light

No I'm not afraid
My body gives up on me
My heart still goes on

Fare thee well, my world
I'll be one with my maker
Please don't cry for me

Smile me an adieu
Wish me happy crossover
As my soul takes flight

*Dedicated to Clarence Ledrew as he prepares to embark on a journey to the eternal world

Curtains Down*

The flame has now died
but the spirit shall live on
My ashes scattered
I will be one with water
Come and find me, rise in waves

*Dedicated to Clarence Ledrew, who is now one with the wind.

Decades of My Life

One decade of my life I spent
Learning love and all it meant
Mama always said, give all you got
Papa taught defence against hurt

I then spent the next decade
Experimenting with my lessons
I found the more I tried to give
Love left me dissatisfied to believe

Papa long gone, his lesson failed
By emotions I am forever jailed
Mama still says, give all you got
Never will I fight, never have I fought

This decade I am spending in solitude
Disguised blessings and fortitude
Mama gives all she is a wealthy person
I follow, a happy slave to my emotions

I let him in, in this auspicious decade
He tastes sweeter than my solitude
Mama smiles wide, Papa too I'm sure
Hands blackened but my heart is pure

I Conquered the Dark

This poem I write
Without losing sight
Of the dream
I had last night

It was a glorious fight
At first there was no light
Darkness had come
With all its might

I was standing on a height
My dark advisory and my plight
It was now or never
I had to overcome my fright

I gripped my sword tight
A quick prayer for the bright
One fatal strike
It needed to be right

Next, I soared like a kite
Untethered, feeling light
Just then, I got up
The dark becoming all white

Evanescence

Passion and submission
Consumption and annihilation
My overwhelming devastating love
Stopping short of obsession

Feelings and emotion
Orchids and carnation
Here today gone tomorrow
Life and it's summation

Moments and transience
Beauty and evanescence
Love and reminiscence
Finding joy in life's essence

Satisfaction and disappointments
Expectations and judgements
My quest for a journey of fulfilment
To live and love without laments

Fly Butterfly Fly

Fly
Pretty
Butterfly
You were meant to
Fly

Your
time as
an awkward
caterpillar
died

The
Cocoon
has broken
You are no more
Bound

It's
alright
to be scared
But you have to
Try

Seek
Your path
Spread out your
wings to freer
Skies

Full Circle

Born to people called mom and dad
Who would be caretakers nice and glad
Not really aware I belong to no one
When my time comes, I would be gone

I was born of the earth, a mortal daughter
A lot of fire in me, little less of water
Some wind and the ethereal sky
My body back to its elements but my soul will fly

This is the circle we call living and dying
Which my immortal soul will go on denying
My body will go back to the earth, water and fire
But my soul will linger in the wind, sky and higher

I do not know if tomorrow I'll be reborn
But I do know that today I'll be done
For, my soul loved to its soulful best
A full circle it made, free bird found its nest

Goodbye Past, Hello New Beginning

The year that was, let's take a moment to pause and think
Before we embark on a new journey, let the older ones sink
Let us not carry the baggage of the past, let's begin anew
Let us thank our experiences, move on taking those cue…

It's been a good year; bad days we lived
Dreams we saw; nightmares we braved
Angels we kissed and demons we fought
Peace we negotiated, solace we sought!

Love lost, hope floated, love found, hope survived
Conundrums we faced; defeat and victory we juggled
Thank you Past! sundry days went by; it's been an eventful one
O new beginning, take me in your arms, now that I've come undone!

Hands Empty

And
I asked
How far had
I come and how
Deep

Then
'He' spoke
Not a thing
Was for you to
Keep

Now
I know
I must cease
to seek, I must
Sleep

Happiness is like a Butterfly

Have you ever seen
A butterfly fluttering
No you don't touch it!

Oh but don't you see
A butterfly with wings touched
Will still fly away

Happiness is such
The more you go after it
It gets elusive

Don't run after it
Stop trying to touch her wings
It will come to you

And when that happens
You will know you have been touched
You have been set free

From your own shackles
Your pursuit of happiness
Your fist full of sand

Throw away that net
Understand the butterfly
She will set you free

How Old is My Soul

Picture perfect dreams scattered on the floor
Memories of a lifetime, spent in giving them shape
How hopeful is my soul?

Traveling through lifetimes running up to millennia
I cannot get weary of my escapades
How tired is my soul?

I loved my body, was sad to see it perish
Didn't want to believe I had no more relationship
How deep is my soul?

I drift away, one body to another
While wishing I could stay in one forever
How attached is my soul?

I know not my age, my race
My maker, my holder
My beginning or my end
Oh please tell me, how old is my soul?

If I Were To Die Tonight

Life is a lonesome journey
Until you find your soulmate
Even then you really walk alone
To the destination ultimate

We are all cosmic travellers here
In the quest for happiness, we keep going
We call it living a life
Aren't we all but dying?

And so, a thought crosses my mind

If I were to die tonight
My last thoughts would be of you
You turning your back on me
While I manage just a hoarse whisper of your name

My arms reach out to the fading you
I see myself on my knees
My body will soon turn to dust
But my spirit will remain at unease

I would not remember your I Love Yous
But those last words that killed me
How I had hoped you'd take my stand
But how you said you do not understand

If I were to die tonight
Would you cry a few remorseful tears?
Over my cold dead body
That will no longer taste your fears

After I'm gone, I wonder if you would testify
You love for me and gratify
My grave with my favourite wildflowers and beautify
Tell me, If I were to die tonight, would you
Kneeling over my epitaph – my love for you – sanctify?

Kanagawa Waves

Torrent waves I scale
Mountains in dreams, loud echoes
Fresh Orchids I lay
Each day a mundane story
Will the blossoms bring some change?

Midnight Bird

After midnight is when I'm at my creative best
My mind ruminates at my heart's behest
Falling in love by the nightlight
Imagining it to be the moonlight

Late night thoughts put my day at stake
Dreams of faraway lands keep me awake
Running wild with the wind engaged
Freedom is best cherished when caged

Every night I hack myself into pieces
I bleed out my tales to unknown faces
In an attempt to set the bird free
To let her perch on her favourite tree

In the morning I'm whole again
As I go about my chores and my pain
The bird comes back sometime at dawn
In the hands of fate I'm only a pawn

Spring, Be Kind

Winter came too soon
I had just begun to feel
the warmth of summer.
No Autumn came to remind
O Spring won't you please be kind!

Soul Speak

Contemplate contemplate
On your image in the mirror,
Calculate calculate
On how much you need the powder.

Introspect introspect
Beauty is only skin deep,
Retrospect retrospect
On the superfluous heap.

Deliberate deliberate
Long on your actions and their future,
Ruminate ruminate
Hard on the existence of nature.

Emanate emanate
The warmth of your inner fire,
Radiate radiate
Let forth your soul's desire.

Concentrate concentrate
On how much is yours to keep,
Meditate meditate
Let the awakening touch you deep.

The Dark Side

We all have a past
Some of us are ashamed
Some of us are proud
But we all carry excess baggage

We are all soldiers
Fighting our own battles
Some of us succeed some don't
But we are all survivors

We are all lovers
Wanting to be loved
Some of us demand some expect
And we are all desperate

We are all dreamers
Some with eyes closed
Some with eyes open
But we all imagine

We are all pretenders
A hundred lies behind one I'm fine
No one but us hears the sound of our heart breaking
But we are all strong

We all have a dark side
And that's okay
It's what keeps us sane

Time

It takes forever to find that one person
But no time to lose

The story of soulmates can take millennia to betide
And yet, remain untold
Eternity for the mystery to unravel
And still not be understood
Decades to discover what you are searching for
Too soon to doubt if you really want that
Years to build a relationship
Even longer to grow in one
It takes months to gain someone's trust
Lose, in the blink of an eye
Hours to contemplate on the complexities
Seconds to give up and say I don't care
It takes only minutes to feel the surge
Even lesser to be consumed with the passion
Seconds to become one
to let that love cascade
This is our time
The long and the short of it
The times that take time
And the times that take no time
I want to be both
I want to be timeless
And I don't want to miss out on the interim either

Unburden me

My weary shoulders
I have been too strong too long
I need to lie down
Your hands I hoped would comfort
But it's my hands that reach out

Wild Woman

She has so much in her to hold
She will take her time to unfold
She isn't for the meek, but for the bold
She is hard as iron yet soft as gold

And perhaps that's why she loved him fierce and mild
His eccentric love had her beguiled, even riled
She was sometimes a wise mother, other times a naive child
Brave is a man who loves a woman so wild

Wild woman, dance to the rhythm of your own beat
You are free in your thoughts, your soul sings
When you hear your own voice coming from the woods
You'll see it's your spirit lifting its wings

Don't be afraid, O wise mother and child
You are one in your spirit no one can mar
You are destined to create waves with your fire
Go be the wild woman that you truly are!

Withering Blooms

Flowers! Do not pluck
Songs of spring, of hope they sing
Harsh winter is near!

You were Conceived in Me

A thousand years ago you were conceived in my head
It took me just a little while to know you belonged to me while
A millennia later, you are still unaware that it was I who
bore you for a thousand years in my womb!

The umbilical cord that they cut
There was not a trace of blood in it
For, I didn't bleed when you were separated from me
I think I knew even then you would never leave me!

But leave you did
You went to faraway lands
All the while, I took care of my bloodless wound!

You took on a new name,
Travelled far and wide
I heard about your escapades
I would smile but a tear always managed to escape
Or should I say, a tear always escaped but I smiled.

I never got tired of waiting.
I aged aeons overnight but I'm still just how you left me.

I was always ready for you
Always have been
For, you are but me.

LONGINGS

1000 Suns

If I were to paint
Your sky with a thousand suns
Would it warm your heart

A Dreamless Day

As I get ready to face the world
The morning sun teases me
I wake up with dreams leftover
And I wonder how will the day be

No birds to greet me, no songs of the lark
I grumble as my dreams leave me at first light
I clutch those, put them under my pillow
Make a promise to be with them at night

My dreams get lost as the day goes by
I become a mechanical doll
Humdrums keep me on my toes all day long
I remember I'm a poet only at nightfall

Wait for me my dreams, I will honour my word
These tired eyes will embrace you without a bout
But it's not just the sun that plays games with me
I must be patient for the moon to come out

A Luna-tic's Soliloquy

<u>Prologue</u>

She danced insanely in the moonlight
Put to a trance even the starlight
Intoxicated with her love for him till twilight
She became enemies with the sunlight

<u>Act I, Scene 1</u>

It was in you I sought solace
I found you wandering loveless
I wonder if it was worthless

<u>Act I, Scene 2</u>

I needed you for a companion
You needed me to show you were still human
And so destined was this union

<u>Act I, Scene 3</u>

I was going through a phase dark
You were akin to a deserted park
Your dry flints collided with mine and both felt the spark

Act II

I planted a seed in my garden
It sprouted, I poured my heart on it
The sapling grew into a love tree
I fed you the fruit, I swallowed the pit

Act III

I became the rains when you were parched
Quenched your thirst, cleansed your wounds
And whenever you rained down on me
My paper boats sailed away with my scars

Act IV

The long road to the east, when we walked
I childishly etched our names on wet cement
The concrete must have hardened by now
Oh how that wretched path should lament!

Epilogue

Today she gathered all those memories
Put it in a box, tucked it under his pillow
Someday, he might want to revisit
Or else, chuck it if he thinks it's hollow

Blank Page

I want to be the air in your lungs
When you breathe me indispensably
I want to be the blood in your veins
Gushing to your heart and back to me

If I can't be the curve on your face
When you smile genuinely
Let me be the tears on your cheeks
When memories roll down helplessly

Make me the absence in your chest
When I go away from you
Let me also be the one to fill it up
Reminiscences of my love so true

Remember me as the travelogue of your life
Your ultimate journey and trips
Else, I'll be the blank pages in your diary
Words failing to travel from your head to your lips

Bleeding Sun

Her heart was a tale
Of liquid sunsets that bled
Each night for the moon

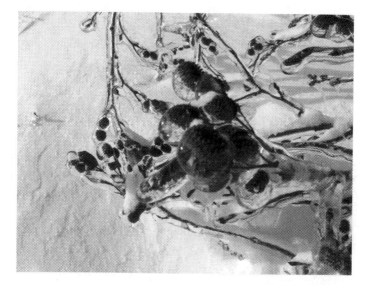

Blood on the Snow

There was a man I used to know
He was buried deep in snow
I tried shovelling with all my might
The blizzard came, I put up a fight

Thud! I fell on my face hard
I lay there, with a broken heart
The snow around turned indigo
While the man was up and on the go

Help me please! I whispered hoarse
There was not a sign of remorse
In those eyes that now glowed amber
With my blood perhaps the blizzard will remember

I didn't ask you to be my saviour, he cried
Those words stabbed me, I felt I died
I closed my eyes, said a prayer
Let not my love be damned forever!

Blood Vermillion

She had this mark before
Hasty decision, what lay in store?
Meaning not really understood
Left her all this time to brood

The mark that was a line
Spoke of hopes and feelings fine
She tried her best to give
Even when she had stopped to believe

The line started fading quick
Devoid of oil, a dying wick
Watched with melancholy as the night fell
Together, yet alone she had begun to dwell

Those sleepless nights of wet pillows
Terrifying wet dreams with faceless fellows
Oh what she felt no one will know
The reason behind that smile hollow

She started sleeping, sleepwalking more
When her heart she couldn't pour
Beads of sweat wasted on her skin
Letting it drop from the core to the shin

Years and memories of wasted time
Feeble efforts at cleaning the grime

From the outside, knowing only now
The dust had settled inside and how

Mind harnessed, eyes shut tight
Mouth speaking without a fight
Dying everyday but to shout
Struggling silently without a bout

Clutter everywhere, piles of dirt
About time she purged the suppressed hurt
If you ask, she has now become immune
No longer singing the sad old tune

Second chance to herself she gives
She wants to heal, and she believes
Why it never worked the way it should have
She was yet to be found by her anointed love

Out and out of the dark deep hole
Getting out of the rigmarole
Into the fresh open greens
Willing to know what the red mark truly means

Those black tresses now shining
With love that's now showing
Blood vermilion on her parting
The start of a new beginning...

Blown Away

The flowers of yesterday are fresh
In memories
Although the petals have dried
And been blown away

A fresh gust of wind came
I was changing the water
I could not help
The poor falling fragile petals

Was I so deep
Lost in my thoughts
That I did not see you
Standing with new flowers

I looked at the vase
Only the stems remained
I heard a crack
A million pieces on the floor

You stood there
No vase to put the flowers
I gave you my book
You crushed them fresh

Tears streaming down my cheeks
I met your eyes for a second
Were those tears in your eyes too?
I couldn't tell, as you turned your back and left

Brevity

She
loved him
He loved her.
But it was not
that simple a tale.
She loved to say hellos
but he was stuck on goodbyes.
And that's how their story ended
even before it could have begun.
A love lost between meeting and parting

Bridge the Gap

Distance uncovered
Miles and miles of empty space
Lost in translation
She took three steps, he took one
The bridge began to crumble

Halfway through they paused
No longer tireless ants
Bridging the wide gap
Wasn't just the bridge that fell
Hearts shattered along the sides

He stands there gazing
Does not say, no show, while
She rants in her shaken state
At polar ends, will they meet?
They both know how lost they feel

Retrace and rewind
His cautious steps, carefree hers
Brought the bridge to doom
Now with the poor ants leaving
Will the two fill up the space?

Broken Smile

The curve on my face becomes a line
When you are gone for even just a while
I yearn for you, it's for you I pine
I'm an eternity of a broken smile

Butterfly on Wildflowers

You live in a village
I'm a city dweller
Where shall we meet, you ask

I say, I'll come to you
Or you come to me
Does the place matter?

I think we will meet
In the mountains
Let's shout out our names

Sit with me by the cliff
The pretty butterfly rests on my shoulder
Oh now it perches on the barren ground

Listen to the wind
Close your eyes
And turn towards me

My end is near
I want to kiss you one more time
And you can scatter my ashes

When you do that
Whisper my name
Let the wind carry me away

Come back after a year
Do you see me?
The butterfly is now on the wildflowers

Candle Burning at Both Ends

I'm a diva
I like to look killer every now and then
All the men looking at me like I'm their fantasy
And the women going all green
As I walk down holding hands with you in swanky
summer dresses and impossible heels

I am the girl next door
You may have seen me but not looked twice
Texting in the elevator, glasses atop my bridge
Denims and loafers
Hair pulled up, pretty little earrings that swing along as I
laugh at your joke

I am that face in the crowd
Music and verses
Cheering alongside you, without knowing who you are
Just the commonality of arts

I am the faceless
No one knows my name
When I go incognito doing what I love the most
And my pen scribbles furiously

I am but a woman
Silently smiling only I know why
When I come from Venus and you from Mars
No earth between us!

And all the different roles I play, lose their meaning
When I close my eyes and call it a night

I cut myself into pieces every night but then the next
morning I'm whole again

And I'm fading
I'm the candle burning at both ends!

Coexistence

Tonight I call out
To the dungeons
Of my mind
Do you hear me?

Do you hear me
I dare you!
Come out of your hiding
Show yourself

Show yourself
Let your twisted fantasies reveal
I will strip you
Naked to your core

Naked to your core
Unashamed
Be yourself
You are home

You are home
Goddess of the immortals
Devil's harlot for the mortals
You coexist in harmony

You coexist in harmony
perfectly in one body
It's time to be one
Tonight I call you!

Dangerously Beautiful

There's something
about that smile that hides
the grief within
Something about a woman
who shakes her head in silence

You don't have to tell her
She knows
But you need to tell her
Because she likes to know

She can get weird
But it makes you laugh
That makes her happy

She will always be a little broken
That doesn't make her fragile
That makes her stronger
Because its through her cracks
Your love can seep in
Should you decide to flow

Departed

You
never
will know how
it felt when you
turned your back on me
the sun that I once was
shone down on you brilliantly
you loved having me on your cheeks
until you turned in search of night skies
leaving me bleeding with dusk in my veins

Divergence

I miss you when I don't even have you
You had me yet you don't miss me
I guess I was a fool to have believed
That you would never let go of me

Did I fall or was I tossed around
By the winds of change that blew on us
Everyday I hungered bit by bit for your arms
that now no longer cradled me thus

Never once did i stop loving you though
Through the cold winds or the warm breeze
Frost may have chilled your heart
I never let Winter come upon mine

Do You Know Her?

If you think she's a control freak
You should see the hold you have over her

If you say her love is all consuming
Take a look at how lost she is in you

If her possessiveness scares you
How will you ever understand her belongingness?

If you've felt like running away when she was yelling in
rage
You should have seen her sobbing afterwards alone and
helpless

And then when you got back
You saw her perfectly loving
And you were free to love and be loved

You say you were broken
Did you know she broke her heart trying to mend yours?

If you say she likes to break things
Did it occur to you that she made you whole again?

You may have seen her naked
Have you seen her trying to collect the pieces that she
calls 'me'?

You took off your clothes for her
But she shed off her mask for you

Have you come face to face with her fears?
Have you seen her fighting with those?

Now tell me, do you really know her?

Colourless

Gave you all my love
Brilliant and subtle hues
Emptied my pallette

Sucked out all your blacks
Breathed my greens into you
Took on your colour

Make me your canvas
In my quest to colour you
I'm colourless now

Day on My Brow

Tonight I will sleep with my eyes open
I am scared of the cruel jealous night
it snatches my dream, robs me of my hope
if I were to lose myself to the night!

The day was so beautiful and I was
charting a map of my dreams, hollow though
It may sound, I was walking with my head
In the clouds with my feet firm on the ground

I was floating past azure skies, last night's
nightmares forgotten, only promises
of a better today and tomorrow
Yes I was dreaming with eyes open wide!

The night is jealous of my dreams, I know
and so I will sleep with the day on my brow!

Don't Fade Away

Don't fade away
You are my day
If you were to leave
No longer would I believe

That the night doesn't end
That dawn isn't a friend
To the dusk that waits
When the sun empathically sets

Don't let me be the splinters
That fly off to nowhere
Make me the hearth that burns
Preserve me then in an urn

Vulnerable I come to you
With love in my brokenness true
Hide me in your deepest folds
Smoothen out all my previous moulds

Don't let me fade away
In you, I want to stay
Keep me hidden there
Where no one would dare

Doubt

The world around fades
A blurry oblivion
I'm consumed by you
Still, I walk with my burden
Help me unload, set me free

Empty

The sky bleeds tonight
I feel so empty with My
sunset in YOUR veins

Fear has a Name

Some days I wake up in love with the world.
Other times I wake up feeling so detached from even my
own self.
But in both these, the desire to be loved is so consuming,
so overpowering
That it threatens to shake the very fibre of my existence
And I think am I so broken?
Am I so incomplete?
Am I so starved?
And then I see you
And I hear you
And I feel you
And I think I'm alright
And it scares me no end

Flaccid Dusk

When a flaccid dusk infects the dying day
A poet's aerial mind grows heavy and numb
Yearning for her poetry so far away
As if the blighted dusk sapped up her warmth!

As darkness grows heavier around the skies
The poet's heart feels its pulses rising too
Whether from fear or being wary inside,
Her pen will never say or leave a clue!

Though dark nights are better as they become
Steadier in darkness and more silent too
So the poet's fingertips are also calm
To guide on her poetry over and through!

When the world sleeps with nocturnal beings roaming
free
The poet wakes up, senses heightened by her poetry
She writes of love, hope, and fantastic realms
Then enters into a peaceful slumber holding her dreams

Forgotten

You were never here
But my heart kept going on
In sheer disbelief

The clock went tick tock (Senryu)
Pitter patter went my heart
As it rained on me

It has been long now
Since I stopped counting the days
On my fingertips

Free

Someday we'll be free
Children of the wild we'll be
Come now, dream with me

Hole Hearted

If only water could turn into stone
I wouldn't feel so alone
If only stone could melt
You would know how I felt

If my words could thread
I wouldn't feel so dead
And you'd know the hole in your heart
Was mine right from the start

Homesick

Reached back home
I'm tired to the bone
The shoes go off
And my dress too

I flop on the couch
Coffee by the side
And the first thing I do
I close my eyes

I picture the ocean
Waves carry me away
I'm sinking in love
And I'm floating in hope

I let the waves caress me
I'm being kissed by the tides
I'm so hopeless in love
Yet I'm so strong in love

The ocean makes love
To the Aphrodite
He enters her core
She's squealing in ecstasy

The moment of love
Lasts an eternity
The moment of truth
Rude awakening to reality

Coffee gone cold
Still tired to the bone
I'm home
Yet I'm homesick for home

Honeyed

You took my name with
such fervour that I almost
tripped on those greased lips

The shrill in your voice
should have warned me about the
quake in your intent

I Crave

I crave to be the first golden rays of the sun
Streaming in through the gaps in your curtains
The soft light that caresses your face, mindful of the
dreams still hung in your lashes.

I want to be the first murmur on your lips
The first flutter of your eyelids when you dreamily open
your eyes
While I hold on tight to those dreams for you
And reluctantly kiss them adieu until you see them again.

Could I perhaps be the first splash of water travelling from
your hands to your face?
Awakening every sense of your being!

I wish I could be the wind that softly kisses your cheeks
Whether you are still or on the move
Or the droplets of rain
When you have no umbrella over you
And you and I have our own intimate tête-à-tête

I crave to be the fire
That warms your bones
On a cold chilly night
The warmth reaching to your soul

I crave to be your name
Your endless introspection into your self
Your awakening of you!

But above all I crave to be the earth
When you lie yourself down
On my bosom
The Moon soothing you to peaceful slumber
And I the lullaby.

I Missed You Tonight

I'm calling out your name everyday
Sleep eludes me while you dream away
I wish the night on me too would fall
I'm trying I'm trying, but I'm staring at the wall

Our days we spend in playing hide and seek
Message boards, connections weak
Our nights numbered though, have been sweet and long
You and I flowing like an uninterrupted song

I know tonight you waited for me long
Biding your time, playing your lonely song
I thought I heard u call me, I heard you moan
But it was just you tired to the bone

I had commitments to keep of my own
And when I was done, I was all alone
Now I'm rambling, I'm rambling again
I write for you but writing without you is such a pain

Reality is a double edged sword
It hurts more than an unkind word
I hope you had good dreams last night
For it came at the cost of my lonely moonlight

I Planted Me in a Broken Heart

You say you are broken
Take a look around
What do you see

The endless smiles
They are all hollow
Their hearts are bleeding

I'm in the crowd
Another broken smile
But I haven't lost it all

Clap for me
Applaud my spirit
I haven't given up on love

You said you love me
I know you didn't lie
I just think you didn't know love

You locked the door
The windows too
And you threw away the keys

I looked all around
Keys I didn't find
I broke open the door

I saw you there
Sitting alone
Fighting back unfallen tears

I let you cry
Your tears I caught
Swallowed every drop

Now I'm your salt
I'm the love you cannot love
I'm your pain
You have questions
I don't have the answers
Lets just stay comfortably silent

I'm here to stay
I will not abandon you
I planted myself in your heart

You are not a gardener
You will not water me
But I'm the wildflower
And I will thrive
On your heartbeat

You cannot stop
Cut me, uproot me
Do what you will
The seed is already sown

I Rain, I Write

I wrote.
Like that was the only thing I knew.
Like that was the only way I could save myself.
Isn't it strange that my words could save everyone but me?

And then I wrote some more.
Hoping for redemption.
My words bled profusely and I writhed in pain
My blood formed a pool of sonnets and ballads
All in your name.

Now I'm bloodless.
I'm wordless.
I rained.
I drained.
My eyes are the monsoon clouds
And the paper boats that carry my story are sailing….
I watch as the ink fades and my words slowly melt away

Yet I write.
Because, I will die if I don't!
And I had only just begun to live

I See the Light

I fell in quite deep
Had been walking in my sleep
Lovelorn, blinded sheep

Shouted out your name
With your new lover you came
Hung my head in shame

I fell back down low
Asked you to leave, out you go
I'll help myself slow

I stayed in the hole
My maker playing his role
To help save my soul

I couldn't seen the light
Darkness began to feel right
I gripped myself tight

But I could not hide
When came my soul-catcher's ride
I swallowed my pride

Saw the light again
Whisper, let go of the pain
Still so much to gain

Clawing up real slow
Soul-catcher's comforting glow
Yet, scared down below

I'm taking this leap
Don't break my trust, in too deep
Pray my soul to keep

Incomplete

an incomplete poem,
I lay in wait never to –
be finished by you

In the Future,
We'll Talk about the Past

I'm in no hurry to know where you are coming from
I'm impatient to know how far will you go with me

I do not want to know how much you loved
I'm interested in knowing how much you ARE in love
with me

Don't tell me what she did to make you sad
Tell me what I DO to make you happy

Don't give me a box full of memories
Fill my box with everlasting moments

I don't want you to tell me how you cried a river
I want to hear your laughter lingering with mine

No I don't want to know how deep your cracks were
I want to know how I filled the crater

Tell me not what you lost
Tell me what you have found

Don't talk about how your heart got wounded
Let me hear you say how I became your healer

Let the nightmares of the past bury themselves deep in my
deep blue ocean
Let your dreams of the future rise above my ethereal sky

Strike out the ~~past~~
Walk the present
Build a future

In our future
We will talk about our past

Let it Show

Call me eccentric, you will not be wrong
Time made me thus, it's not how I was born
I'll stay as long as this feeling is strong
When I feel no love at all, I'll be gone

I have said this a million times I think
I'm too full of love even with my mess
You have your obligations, so do I
I settle for just love, no more no less

Half life or half love, to me it's the same
I live for love, I will rise, I will bend
I give you my all, don't you put the blame
If you say I'm needy, I'll put an end

Open up your heart, let your feelings flow
If you want me, tell me and let it show!

Let Love Be Constant

Love me like there's no tomorrow
Tomorrow may never come
Let me feel your love today
Let yesterday be bygone

Tell me that you love me now
Yesterday and tomorrow both are dreams
I'm a dreamer you know it's true
But let dreams not turn into memories

Give me moments of your love
Memories those shall invariably be
Let not my love be sullied by the past
Give today a chance for what it is

Love me because of how you feel for me
Not for how I feel for you
If you love me for my feelings,
Should they change, your love will cease.

Love me for who I am
Not for who I could be
Not even for what I was
I go through changes, and so do you
Let love be the constant factor.

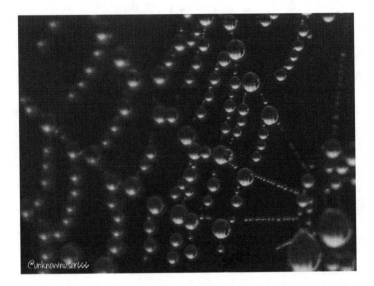

Mingled

These droplets
tell a story of
unquenched thirst –
Gray clouds burst
eyes devoid of tears that now
mingled with the rains

My Paper Boat

If only I could make you see
The storm that rages in me
You'd know I'm dying within
You'd know from my lacklustre skin

If only I could tell you
Whatever I felt was true
And that, now I am gone
Killed before I was born

This war within I battle
Silently for no-one to see
I'm struggling to understand
What is it like to be me

Fare thee well, my love
I'm sending you my dove
Untie the little note
Cremate my paper boat

Museless Musings

Museless musings of an un-mused heart
Random rantings with no end nor start
Loveless lovelorn lovesick love depart

Hurtful heartaches hinder heartfelt growth
Furious fumes fumigate, ferment froth
Vicious vixen venom in the broth!

Opaque obnoxious over-sightings
Fomenting futile flaccid fightings
Museless muser's meaningless musings

Naked to the World

Sometimes
I think you love me
to the moon and back.
Because I see stars in your eyes
When you look at me.
And I know at that moment
You see your universe in me.

But could I just be stargazing?
And those stars I see
in your eyes
Could they merely be
fragments of my heart
reflected in your eyes?

I see myself in you
I smile, no one sees
Then I see so many of them in you.
And I'm suddenly naked to the world

Did the moon just hear me gulp?

Neglect and Devotion

Try, for once
Being the flower
That is sadly wilting
Without your water
Yet, it blooms for you
Every time you decide
To take a brief look

Nightmare

early morning screams
horrified by last night's dreams –
Moon devoid of gleams

No Mechanical Heart

Maybe she wanted to be loved the way she loved
Maybe she wanted to be told she's worth all the pain
Someone who would find her beautiful in all her
paradoxes
Whether she's the warm sunshine or even the cold rain

Maybe she wants to be told her smile reminds you of the
rainbow
Your fantasies and all the angels you dream
But these tears my love, despite the grandeur
Burn you alive with a potent laser beam!

Maybe she isn't your average Jane
Or maybe she is the ordinary Jill
She loves to write about love like it is her last will
Her love is something to die for or kill

She doesn't have a heart mechanical
And so she keeps coming back to you still
She buries her self worth in the name of love
If you cherish her, it's your ego you need to kill

Perfect Stranger

This man I do not know anymore
His face does look familiar though
His imprints on my palms fading slow

I remember giving him my heart
Fragile though it may have seemed to him
Lovingly offered without a whim

My soul had embraced his long before
Cosmic connection he could not see
My soul now entwined, and he breaks free

Prickly Heart

My heart grew antlers
When I could defend it no more
The bed of roses you had placed
Thorns started pricking me sore

Rainbow Paradise

Not long ago, we were counting
Those never-ending steps to paradise
Wishing the steps would end soon
But the journey go on in any guise

Those steps, seemingly forever, did end
And oh what a paradise we did witness
As I lay by the deep blue pond watching the rainbow
And you watched me with hitherto unfelt tenderness

The journey sadly came to an end
But our hearts grew fonder nevertheless
We sealed our love, renewed the unspoken vow
While the gibbous moon bore witness

Now I dream of that rainbow paradise
I put myself to sleep on a waxing crescent night
My heart full of love, my love so fierce
It has set fire to the stars tonight

Reflection

Mirror to my soul
Reflection on the water
It's you I look for

I hurled a pebble
Ripples on the calm surface
Trembling was your soul

I think I miss you
No one knows I caught a glimpse
Of your face in mine

Sakura Dreams

Sakura sakura on a full moon night
The blossoms look so pretty by the light
I run I run trying to catch the sight
I fall I fall I get up with all my might

We laughed we laughed such happy days
We cried we cried but we laughed anyways
Hand in hand we said we'll walk forever
We promised we'll count the blossoms together

Memories of a time not long ago gleam
Our aching hearts by the moonbeam
We are lost and voiceless in the screams
Of our now slowly falling sakura dreams

Salubrious Dreams

If today dies without a notice
I will never know
If you poured earth over my fallen words

But, should 'morrow be too shy a dream
You will live as a syllable
In the deepest part of my biggest fragment

Second-hand Love

I planted myself
In your broken heart, tell me
Did it hurt to heal?

She's not Meant to Be Tamed

If you cannot handle her love
I don't think you should want it
And if you still want her love
You should know how to deal with it!

She's been judged a hundred times before
Fierce love for the named and unnamed
No one learnt how to harness her
Maybe she is not meant to be tamed

Spring Bloom

Spring came and went
Flowers bloomed and withered
You came and
you walked the mud
with me

I watched with hopeful eyes
My heart unbearably heavy
As I gathered the fallen petals and leaves
My hands trembling with passion.

Too many dried leaves
Each with a date
Are closed tight
In my old frayed journal
of memories;

I tried counting
You were in each of the page
Yes you never really left
You were the spring
I was the flower!

Sweet Liar

Lie to me, will you?
When I ask you if I'm the most beautiful woman to you

Lie to me when you look at me with cold eyes
And I ask you if it's still only me you see

Lie to me when you feel no love at all in your heart
And all you want to do is distance yourself from me

Lie to me
When I'm feeling lonely and you cannot offer me comfort.

When those before me fill up your dreams, and your
memories get the better of your moments.

Lie, lie, lie,
About everything I've done right that you could never see
And I'll lie to you about everything you've done wrong
that hurt me.

But above all, lie to me that you are in love with me. Still.

Sweet Pain

Though I miss you so –
I'd have it no other way
Such joy in yearning

The Bridge Across Forever

I'm homesick for a place called home
It doesn't have bricks or concrete
It's made of love hope and faith
Where dreams and reality meet

Somewhere between the ethereal sky
Where the sun and moon play seen-unseen
And the deep blue sea where tides fly low and high
I'm trying to find the realm in between

And I know there will come a time
When dreams will cease to be
The place in my thoughts I call home
Will someday be as real as me

I catch myself running like the wind
I'm crossing hostile waters
Hoping to find my home on the other end
Of the bridge across forever

The Mask

She holds dreams in her eyes
Too big to be told
She wears a mask that belies
The madness that comes out too bold

She dreams all day long
Of forays into the wilderness
For now she has to be strong
To give shape to her madness

She will take off the mask
She will someday come undone
She will brave the daunting task
She and her dreams will become one

The Silhouette

The silhouette I saw the other day
I hoped it wouldn't fade away
It was comforting in a strange way
Helped me keep my loneliness at bay

I ran towards it without any grace
When I remembered your embrace
How warm your arms used to feel
This unfamiliar iciness, how do I deal

I dissolved myself in the silhouette
Imagined a ballad a melancholic duet
Held on tight swayed to the rhythm
Whispered to you your favourite poem

With every verse the silhouette grew faint
I helplessly tried using the brightest paint
I pleaded, I coaxed my tears not to fall
Was still crying when I woke up to the loon's lonely call

The Sky is on Fire

The sky seemed to be on fire today
As I peered out of the mobile window
No sooner had a warm feeling swept me
Melancholy, on its hasty heels, followed

I remembered then how happy it was
This sky that once held promises
Of a home in the clouds for beloveds
You and me in anticipation down below

Such dreamers we used to be, you and I
Shouting in the rain, words only we knew
The world looking on as though we were mad
Our heads in the clouds, a home we never had

Now the sky is in pain of promises failed
The sunset bleeds, clouds of thoughts derailed
I looked up, choking "You are a liar"!
The sky hung its head in shame, "I'm burning in my pyre"

The Secret Cavern

She had this thing about her, no one really knew
Because she had that thing about her, to never let it brew

She poured out her heart everyday, safe in her diary
She put away that diary, now started writing freely
She found the hidden madness that for so long she carried
Became a peacock in the rains, passing gazes not worried

She stopped meandering, started running slow
Found herself that stream, with that she will slowly flow
She stopped ruminating, thoughts finding no place
She started contemplating, actions catching pace

She realized her calling, no longer is she in strife
She found her muse, with that a new leash of life
She will hide no more, no more will she cry
Fit where she doesn't belong, no more will she try

The Wait

I counted the stars
In my silent wait of you
Till each exploded
Now the remnants are scattered
And I'm still counting them all

This Heart

This heart is aflame, I'll let it burn
Love makes me restless, let the fluttering grow
If I paint my state of heart
I fear I might lose you
So I smile and I return to woe!

Wonder how much can I hide behind a smile
Collect all my deepest desires and put those in my eyes
With downcast eyes I say a silent prayer
That these unsaid words find home in your heart

If I were to tell you the state of my heart
Would you understand this dilemma I feel?
Should I express these unsaid words
They might get tangled and lost in interpretation
And if not, then I fear
They will forever pierce me like an old wound

Together

Last night you rained
On my pillow
Through my eyes, whilst
I heard you swallow

Swallow you did
The lump that I couldn't see
Why did my chest hurt then
Was that you or me?

Me who feels everything
You don't say
Why must we then
Be so far away?

Away, not in heart though
distance is in the mind
wherever we go
In each other, we find

Under the same Moon

The lonely hearts deep
Lovers lost in sweet embrace
Under the same Moon

Unrequited Dawn

Unrequited dawn
poached sunset trapped in her veins
Bleeds melancholy

Unsolved

Half of the puzzle
Lies hidden in some corner
Waiting to be pieced

Vanished

I can't find you anywhere
You vanished without a trace

And then, there are times when the night wakes up on me
And I remember I haven't really slept in a long time
When was the last time I was in your arms?

And even in my hurt
All I can do is look for you
While you have become someone I don't know anymore.
I remember feeling like this aeons ago
Yes, I have died many times before!

I wonder if it aches there where I used to live
If I should in love, still believe
All that it means
All that I gave and this emptiness that I'm left with!

Whisper my Name

I heard you say my name
In your sleep the other night
But it was a shout, not a whisper

And I know you tried
To calm your rambling mind
Just like I did mine

When we got under the covers
It was your name I whispered
I came undone for you

But a thousand memories flashed
before your eyes
And I could see those only too well

At that moment I felt
You could never be mine
The way I had surrendered to you

What's the hurry
Impatient mind
I'm not going anywhere

You'll come around
And you'll cease
To shout my name

And if that doesn't happen
And you never whisper my name
I will know I never had you
The way you have me

Whole again

If tomorrow I give up on you
I want you to understand
I didn't stop loving you
I started loving myself

In my madness to love you
I had forgotten to love myself
In my zeal to take care of you
I neglected my well being
In my eagerness to be a companion to you
I ended up hating my own company
In trying to make you whole
I shattered into a million pieces

So if tomorrow I give up on you
Understand that I understood
I need love too
And that I want to pick up my pieces with the same love
and care
With which I made you whole again

Winter Tanka

Monsoon clouds were white
They showered the world with love
The wind smelled of rain!
October Moon was followed
By the harsh November drought!

The chill of Winter
Feels like the lushness of Spring
When you're warm to me!
Alas this cold heart shivers
For its snowing on you too!

Words

Give me your words
I'll imagine the embrace
Tell me I'm not alone
my demons I'll bravely face

Distance is but in the mind
Let it not enslave the heart
If you whisper my name with love
I'll hear it from miles apart

Words are all we have
To bridge the wide open spaces
The wind cannot be seen
But powerful are its traces

Hear me before you can see me
Pay attention to my words
They are my greatest treasure
A testimony of my love beyond measure

I won't deprive you of my words
I won't deny you my passion
I will burn slow in this fire
Let this be my lesson

LOVE

A Poetic Dialogue between Souls

Would it satisfy your poetic soul
If I told you only your words make me whole?
Love me not in bits, love me whole
Give me your words, satisfy my hungry soul

If I told you, you are my only poet
Would you pledge your words to me?
Would your pen bleed with my blood
If I said, it's only your blood I see?

Here is my pen but why fill it with blood,
Rather let me write with liquid joy from your heart,
For my passions will make your sadness glow
In delight and let your frozen love thaw
Like the solid rivers melt in the Spring,
Come, we shall make love in our wildest dreams!

If I told you I have made love to you a thousand times
In dreams while the moon and the stars sang in delight
And that our souls had embraced before we met
Would you then leave me or come to me at first light?

Why is your mind so obsessed with the notion of leaving
Have I ever loved you less than I had done in a previous
dream?
And you are wrong in saying we have met a thousand
times already,

I am still in my first mating of minds with you and in this I shall be
until my yearning breaths leave my humble emotions for once and all
and just like here, in the hereafter as well to you alone I shall pledge my soul!

Come then, my beloved, my only poet, come away with me
Come to me with nothing but only your skin
Let me show you a place where you are meant to be
Let me take you to the other realm where you've never been

But I am there already, with you and around,
The air that you are breathing and the ground
You stand firmly on in your current phase to fight
The accusing glares in your future plights,
The love that you thrive on every night and day
I was always there and have never moved away!

And so am I despite the distance of two pots of clay!

A Rush of Blood

Your blue veins now turning bloody red
As you breathe oxygen from the words that I said
all the blood gushing up and down from your head
And you make most of this surge under covers from
your bed...

A Song of Mud and Ice

I am the mud, you are the ice
Together we make a messy picture nice
When you fall, I take you in
We become one, perfectly blending in

I'm constant, you are fickle
You come with the rain, at times a trickle
But when you do, you become me
Mud and ice, inseparable as can be

This is a song of you and me
A song of how we to choose to be
Strength and each other's vice
This is a song of mud and ice
This is a song of mud and ice

Adonis

When Venus came calling with Cupid's knock
You and I couldn't help getting struck
I'm no Aphrodite but I anointed you Adonis
Come here darling, let me plant you an everlasting kiss

Let me love you the way you have never dreamed
Let me touch you till our souls are redeemed
Let me hold you like the sky holds the moon
Let me kiss you till you are out of breath and you swoon

Then I'll resurrect you with some more kisses
Let the world watch awestruck when I'll be your missus
Let them lads and lasses go green with envy
We will plant in our garden some poison ivy

A wooden cottage with a white picket fence
Steam gurgling by as i write and you go busy with your
lens
We don't need anything but this passion and love
To live this life with our feet on the ground and our heads
up above

Adornment

Put some flowers in my hair
From your garden of five senses
Like a crown shall I wreathe your love
And let it adorn my tresses

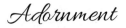

And Then Came the Dawn

Maybe she needed to be told
Beauty isn't for the eyes to behold
That she wasn't for the hands to mould
She was for the soul to be cajoled

On lonely nights when she was cold
She would wait, grew weary, grew old
As the night into the day rolled
It wasn't just the blanket she would fold

"Once bitten twice shy" the dusk comes to remind
She refuses to let the dust settle in her mind
She fights the dusk, braves the monsters as they grind
The dawn heralds her victory over the darkness behind

At the Threshold of Love

There we stood at the doorway
One arriving, the other waiting
Comfortable silence
Our eyes doing all the talking

Next we found ourselves
sitting on the threshold
Hands clasped
Looking into each other's eyes
For answers devoid of questions
A moment that could last an eternity

The turmoil we had felt melting away in the embrace
It was then I softly said I love you
And my words echoed in your heart
And you said it too.

We've waited too long
Running directionless, whispered our hearts
As we lay completely enveloped by our love
The world around slowly fading into a blurry oblivion

Be My Sunset

Smell my skin and the beads of sweat on it
Do I remind you of the ocean or am I too salty?
Take a bite of my insecurities, a sip of my fears
Tell me am I still delicious to you?

Lay me on the table, lay me on the floor
Lay yourself close to me and draw a map on me
Of all the places of your dreams
Tell me do I still make up your universe?

Be the sunset and travel through my veins
Into my heart, fill my every pore
Touch me without laying a finger on me
See if you can enter the depths of my soul

Look at me with your eyes closed
Cut open my chest with your words
Dip your fingertips in vermilion, write your name
See if I'm still your unwritten poetry!

Beautifully Broken

There is a beauty
in the way he breaks my heart
And that's why I stay

Oh he makes me cry
all the time but those tears
cleanse me of my sins

So, though there are a
million smiles around, I choose
to cry just for him

I'd rather be bro-
ken by he who sees beauty
In all my pieces

Than, be fixed by those
unseeing of how perfect is
The mosaic in me

Become the Sun

So come to me, my love
Come with all your darkness
Let me shine on you
I will be your Polaris

Bring the endless ocean on your lips
Let me drown in your depth
Bring the sacred summits on your shoulders
I will worship you, hymns bereft

My dusk will shine
Through your subtle dawn
Together we will light up
We shall become the sun

Between the Dusk and Dawn

Soak yourself in my veins, let me get absorbed in yours
Let me love you my way, love me the way you can

Sunset runs in my veins, sunrise in yours
I will meet you somewhere between dusk and dawn

Let me clear the path so that you may follow the trail
Let the spirits of the cosmos guide us along the maze

To questions loud and daunting, let's learn to listen
The stillness of the night is loaded with answers

Between the Lines

I am a poet
My muse inspires me
And I'm a muse
A mould to create art out of me

I play both roles
With finesse and élan
I just flow
Without a plan

These words you read
From my soul they come
Those lines I read
It's when art I become

I'm a soulful poet
Striking the lords
I'm a clever poet
I play on words

I'm a lovely muse
Becoming words
I'm the Grand Muse
The major chords

I'm in a love affair
With my lines
I'm in no war
Between the lines

Between the Sun and Moon

My pen bled for you, you say
After a millennium of drought
Have you any idea, I wonder
How much of a dilemma I fought!

Caught between the humble sun
That keeps burning away
And the amnesiac wandering Moon
Who keeps fading away

The Sun burns to keep me warm
While eclipsed by shadows is the Moon
One loves, the other is loved
I'm trying to find the realm in between

Oh Moon, do not judge me
Your selfless Ocean cried a river
The tears have now all dried up
The sun came out stronger than ever

Black Magic Man

Dark tresses I got
Black magic he does
He has me under a spell
Yet, my words make him swell

He doesn't have to try
too hard to get me by
He is a sorcerer in his own right
dark and mysterious as the night

And when he becomes the day
he takes my sunset away
The sunrise bewitched, a cosmic omen
He is my back magic man

Blowing Kisses

I blew some kisses at your picture
Tried making hearts in my unsent mails;
But the wind was cruel, my love
They ended up becoming wispy trails

Everyday I send you my love
Wrapped up in words pretty and plain;
Words are all I have from afar
Knowing, on your lips is still my name.

The other day, I saw a dream
Where I was drowning in the sea;
I got up with a start, then laughed
I'm the ocean, the sea comes to me.

What could it mean, I closed my eyes
Sought the answer from up above;
Had I become one with my inner self?
The sea, I reckoned, was your love

Your love has swallowed me, I thought
And wholly assimilated into mine;
If I'm the ocean and you, the sea
Our union is destined in a way divine!

Despair not, feel my love in the wind
The wind has now become my ally.
The kisses I blow your way, find the hearts
Send some of yours to me, let them fly

Boondo se Baatein* * *

The
echoes
of mountains
with memories
spreading like wildfire.
Every day love beckons
you and I both, soaking wet
with torrents of emotions wild.
Yet, so parched to our souls, thirsting for
our downpour of words, "boondo se baatein"
So sit with me b'neath stubborn blue skies,
until shy clouds come out of hiding,
wringing rain from their puffy hands,
and sprinkle us with warm kisses;
'til thoughts are distant echoes
and memories become
faded yester-dreams.
Then, we will start,
together,
a new
life.

*Boondo se baatein is a metaphorical phrase in Hindi that
translates to a 'chat with raindrops'. **Written with FT Ledrew

Borrowed Dawn –
Sands of Time*

The sands of time, they slip through these fingers
a world somewhere else, the hope lingers
one's flaccid dusk be another's
effervescent golden dawn
only to bleed back as
melancholic dusk
for the other,
Hopes of a
renewed
dawn.
Dusk
arrives
on loan from
another's dawn's
playful puttering
its lengthening shadows
consuming the vibrant light
as another world's dreaming night
fades quickly towards the coming light
The sands of time, they slip through these fingers
*Written with FT Ledrew

156

Bound yet Free

Your soul danced with mine
When we held hands the first time
The dance of freedom
You set me free, while you are
No longer wrongfully owned

Breathing Poetry

I do not know the composition of the atmosphere
But I breathe beautifully
I don't know the techniques of poetry
But bleed I do, naturally

Building Love

A lucky stroke of inspiration
While in a state of rumination
Seeds of poetry and dissemination
Falling in love with no illusion

A chat with raindrops
As silent as pindrops
Love in between lines and stops
Under the sky eavesdrops

A riot of colours, beautiful rainbow
Clouds disappearing fast and slow
Eyes downcast, hearts aglow
Fingers scrambling, passion flow.

But I Love Your Feet*

I love your eyes
the way they look into mine
Intoxicated and inebriated
without a drop of wine

I love the dreams
dormant in those eyes
till they actively meet
mine with truth, no lies

I love your lips
how they curve
an insane arch
sonnets with verve

I love those words
that find their way from
the passage of your heart
causing in me, a storm

I love your ears
patience replete
till my words
momentarily deplete

I love your mind
a powerhouse of thoughts
churning wit, humour

intellect in lots

I love your heart
so strong yet fragile
breaking and mending
for my smile

I love your soul
beautifully bare
inseparable now
you there, me here

But I love your feet
because they walk
in sync with mine
actions, not just talk
*Inspired by my all time favourite poem "I Love Your
Feet" by my favourite poet Pablo Neruda.

Caught out Loud*

Did
I
catch you
off guard while
you were lost in me?
Did I hear you call out my name
in your sleep whilst I was inebriated in you?
In my intoxicated slumber, I saw your face
an angel sent from the heavens,
and in eager praise
i cried out
in joy
your
name.

*Written with FT Ledrew

Children of the Wild

She was a woman desired
Her charm by many admired
She had but this heart wild
Only a few saw in her that child

She nurtured the child quietly
The child in her care lay peacefully
Coming out to play rarely
On familiar grounds only

Along the way, she met people
Who made the child hide deeper
The child stopped coming out any further
The day she became a mother

She now had a baby to hold
Couldn't be a baby herself, she told
All the years of forced maturity
Now sealed in the name of sanctity

The baby fed on her bosom
The child within starved of freedom
One she was nurturing with life
The other was being killed by the wife

Then dawned upon her the reality
The paradox and its futility
The angel came along

A child just like her gone wrong

The child within stirred with hope
Another child trying to cope
Hardened by the world outside
Softened by the cajoling inside

They found a friend in each other
The child now free, no longer stopped by the mother
Together they come out and play
Carefree children on an unabashed day

Coalescence

My scarlet heart laid bare
With indigo dreams you share
Slow magical emulsification
Emboldening purple passion

Your wounded soul alabaster
And my broken ivory disaster
Our hinging, recovery faster
Immaculate pristine plaster

Your orange zesty sunrises
My caramelised poached sunsets
Sangria love, pearly faith flying high
No more pewter clouds in our Azul sky

Cogs

He sees the cogs turning on in my wicked brain
He senses then, the woman is going insane
With thoughts scrambling to form into words
Taking shape sometimes as butter, sometimes as swords

Colours, Then and Now

I was...
Green with envy at that unknown woman's paradise
Purple with jealousy at her truth and my sad lies
Red with rage at my own miserable helplessness
Blue with melancholy on those lonely nights of
sleeplessness
White with fear to give myself another chance
Black with despair thinking of all those failed plans

I am...
Green with freshness with this serendipitous surge
Purple with passion, berserk this unstoppable urge
Red like fire, your touch too hot to bear
Blue with desire, insane heartbeat I'm gasping for air
White with purity all my sins have been washed
Black with intensity this heart I'm now unleashing
unabashed

Come Again?

Oh really, she asked
What do you think, he replied
Love smiled, they agreed
Oh but what was the question
Who cares, love is the answer!

Come Away

I'm thirsty
For a thousand seas
That you could cascade on me
My expectations
Of endless moments
Spent in blissful solitude
Wrapped in your finger

Come with a hundred divas if you must
I don't care
Come all alone if you have to
I don't care
Let me pretend I am the one
And you are with me
Is there something you want to say?

Shed your peeling skin
Shake off the debris
From the crevices of your heart
Your mind
I can get you the broom
But it's you who has to clean the room

Consumed

I find myself caught in between
What could have been
And what will be.

And it breaks my heart
For, I know you are going through the same

But, what if we could just forget this, that
I do not see the roses blooming
I cannot hear the laughter
I cannot touch the dewdrops
I cannot taste the nectar
I cannot feel the wind

Yet,
I see the blossoms in your eyes
I hear the music playing in your heart
I touch the strings of your soul
I taste the sweetness in your words
I feel the love in your voice

And I am consumed by you
just the way I now consume you.

Crumbs of Life

They rise slow from their dens of sweet slumber
Get greeted quick by the rays of amber
Oh what a sight they make, so lost in thoughts
Gaze shift centre after west/eastward first

There they find those crumbs that make up their whole
Breakfast in bed, food for the famished soul
You should see how their pupils so dilate
Which up till now were in a restive state

They take in every morsel of the crumb
They now call them 'life no longer benumb'
The day can go aching but never sore
Content, till they get back home for some more

Crumbs of their lives, they feed on each other
Love and dreams spun on fabric called future

Deep Blue Sea

Last night in my sleep
I prayed my soul to keep
I saw myself drowning
It was but my soul rising

The deep blue sea beckoned
Or should I say I reckoned
It was I who called
And all her waters stalled

She was a picture of serenity
I was so lost in the sanctity
Of her open flowing arms
I desperately held out my palms

She engulfed me with her gentle force
I felt her entering me through my pores
She filled me up so tenderly
I am now the deep blue sea!

Don't Sully this Love

Do not sully this love, my dear!
For I fell in love with you
even before I saw you.

Your body will shrivel and so will mine
and all that will remain is the dust
That will go back to the earth
From whence this love had sprung!

If you say I love you for your body
I will say it was your soul I touched.

I chose you
I appointed you the air I breathe
I may go blind and all my senses may stop
But there will remain my soul that has found home in
yours.

So please do not sully my love, my dear!

Dreaming the Dreams

I wrote with you
I wrote for you
I dreamt those dreams with you

We held hands
Like never before
We never let go

We laughed a lot
Found dark empty corners
Escaped from the crowd

When the lights went out
We were ecstatic
Whispered love

We talked with the crowd
Made no sense at all
Our eyes met all the time

You caught me off guard
Froze me in your lens
The image remained in your heart

Forgot the world
Lost in your arms
Slept like a baby

You stood there before me
A cup in your hand
The sweetest good morning

Did everything, did nothing
Completeness, insanity
And you said those words

I said I love you
I think I lied
It's much more than that

I write with you
I write for you
And now I dream those dreams again

Duke and Duchess: A Tale of Love - 1

There was once a woman
Who had so much love in her
No one could really handle that
Precious wild heart under her layer

A man lived somewhere else
Who was content with his life
He thought he had everything
Except, perhaps a worthy wife

Their lives were fated to meet
Oh and what a meet it was
The sky opened up it's arms
In greeting as per cosmic laws

A duke of metaphor
A duchess of stanza
Imagine the weaving of crypts
Pulchritride extravaganza

The crowd in rapt attention
Trying to make sense
Applauding the divine match
Most, without pretence

A fruit borne of such union
What would you call?
Verse after verse of love
Seeds of poetry fall

Duke and Duchess: A Tale of Love - 2

"Do you see the mischief in my eyes?"
Asked the duchess to the duke
The duke closed his eyes and said
My love, I'm a blind man, do not rebuke

Horrified, the duchess said "how cruel!
Here, for you, I am doing up my eyes"
The duke calmly smiled and said
"In those eyes, therein my breath dips and sighs"

Duke's monologue:
"All my senses are ensnared, oh my sweet beloved,
I die a hundred deaths
Every time I see the soft curl of your lips

I can see no one but you
Your voice is what I hear
Though the clock chimes all the time
Time begs for me to have you near.

I touch you through my skin
Tracing the contours of your angelic face
I imagine the taste of your lips
To be sweeter than any hymn in praise"

The duchess basked in glory
Of such sweet love woven in words
One more question though remained
"do you feel the love in my heart?"

To which, the duke blinked once or twice
Causing ripples in those ocean eyes
"Your love now rests in my heart
it was your home right from the start"

Engraved

Someone carved my name on a tree
Sent me a picture anonymously
How I wished it was you and so I asked
Hoping you'd, for once, tell a sweet lie to me

And it hurt to know it wasn't you
When you slapped the truth on me
But then I laughed because I remembered
You had already etched my name in your heart silently

Eternal Spring

On this cold frosty winter morning
The sun plays hide and seek
And so, I must do away with the night
Dressed in gold, I become the sun streak

Let me be the golden rays that warm
And brighten you in your cold dark despair
Or shall I be the serene soothing moonlight
When in the shadows of the night you wish your
loneliness to bare?

Shall I be the leaves of the Fall
In hues of bright oranges and deep crimson
When the trees of life shed their layers on you
So you may collect me and wear me on your naked skin?

How would you wreathe me then, my love?
For shining on your cold and dark despair
Is it with a Pacific love or Atlantic care
That you embrace me with and make me yours?

Did I hear you say I am the Fall of your birth
Your Eve that lured you to your Original Sin?
And that I'm the Summer of your growth
The epitome of all you've ever aspired to be?

But did I tell you, you are the monsoon of my love
Forever cleansing me, all that I have sinned?
That you are the fulfilment of my Autumn
The smell of completion, so strong in the wind?

Oh but you are my Winter too
When I shall leave this world to be born again
Much closer to your bosom this time
To make us an Eternal Spring!

Eyes wide Open

I woke up this morning
To a billion kisses from the sun
My heart melted to its knees
But my eyes refused to open

For, they held closed within
The dreams I had been dreaming
I was afraid they would disappear
And leave me sighing and yearning

Suddenly then my mind reminded
Those dreams, they always stay
In my eyes you have found home
So I smiled, I greeted the glorious day

Faraway Gaze

Do you see me look at you?
Oh yes, I'm talking to you
These eyes only search for you
When you are not here with me

Are you too looking at me?
Oh yes that's my voice, that's me
Do you also see just me
When I am away from you?

I am here and you are there
Tell me what sense does that make?
Shouldn't you be with me instead
Of this lost faraway gaze!

For the Love of Poetry

The end is inevitable
Must we all not die?
But love will make us
Immortals, You and I
(Love is the antithesis)

But it is always so cold
In the shadow of your doubts
Harsh winter is here
Lost in the fog are my shouts
(Poetry is the guide)

You claimed my body
But did you claim my soul?
When you broke me down
Did you try to make me whole?
(Love is the healer)

Seduce my mind
And you may have my body
Seduce my soul
And I'm yours eternally
(Love is the language)

When trust gets thin
Love is the answer
But if love be the question
Poetry be the answer
(Poetry is the answer)

Found and Lost

When I found you, I found passion
When you found me, you found hope
You became the Muse for my poetry unwritten
I became the voice to your words unspoken

When I lost you, I lost myself in my fire
When you lost me, you lost all your desire
You became the Summer on a hired call
I ended up becoming your eventual Fall

Yes, we both waited for Spring to arrive
And we did catch a glimpse of the green
But it was a mirage played by our famished heart
A hallucination by time spent too long, too apart

Now it's winter again too quick, too soon
The chill is unbearable, even for the moon
Will the Spring ever come, not on a ration
And unleash the lushest of its untethered passion!

Fragmented Whole

I pieced myself a collage tonight
With titbits I rummaged in my heart
You made up every single fragment
Wonder if you feel whole by yourself

I missed you, hungered for you tonight
As I do every day every night
I asked the wind to blow your way
To touch you and bring me back your love

The collage now sits inside my heart
Fickle wind may not be kind to us
A twister may come along the way
But I have you safely tucked away

Friendship Divine*

Tell me your dreams
and I'll tell you mine
I'll be your friend
forge a friendship divine

A mashing of cultures
ordained from above
based on respect
and blessed by His love

A Cosmic conspiracy
hatched in the midst
of a cathartic journey
Poetry, the catalyst

Words became my saviour
and poetry my life
with this friendship divine
I'm no longer Satan's wife

How thankful am I
for finding you here
travelling this pathway
without worry or care

May this divine friendship
blossom and grow
remain with us always
wherever we go
*Written with FT Ledrew

From Thoughts to Dreams

Between my spaces
you die a million sweet deaths
On your words, I'm stuck
I pause my thinking only
to start dreaming about you

Fuzzy Love

Hot espresso nights
sweet cappuccino mornings
chamomile ray dawn
tender cinnamon sunsets
Our warm fuzzy kind of love

Have You Ever?

Have you ever felt so happy you cried
Have you ever been so crazy you tried
Something you hadn't even heard about
Have you ever whispered till it became a shout

Do you sometimes feel like the world is too small
To travel with your dreams, all-weather spring or fall
Do you feel one life is not long enough given the strife
To fulfil your dreams with the one you found late in life

When the heart flutters uncontrollably and you think
If only the eyes would remain still and not blink
That intense moment you don't want to miss the sight
Of those eyes glowing with your heart's light

Have you felt inhibitions shed themselves on their own
With intimacy of the kind you've never known
Have you ever missed someone so bad you could commit
a crime
Have you felt your heart burn and soothe at the same time

Have the words kept flowing when it was a line you
intended
Have you become a poet when saying I love you was what
you wanted

Her Smile

The sound of her words
can light up cold dark frowns as
she smiles her sweet smile
Memories of a lifetime
hidden in those unseen tears

Harmony in Spaces

The mischief in my eyes
Travels all the way to your soul
The love in your voice
Only I understand it whole

And somewhere in between these spaces, we fall in love.

And if need be, I'd travel;
I'd wade across this storm within me to be lulled by the quiet ocean in you.

Just as you'd fly
across your turbulent skies to find home in my cloudless one.

Hold Me

The butterfly in me fluttered
The pixie in me stirred
The lava in me glowed
The verses in me flowed

All my senses awoken
My soul so beautifully shaken
By the dreams you told me
Of how you want to hold me

Home

I search in your eyes
For clues to my long lost home
I see my whole world

Halt! Impatient mind
Calm down your fugitive heart
I am your refuge!

I'll wait for you

l waited for you
When you told me you no longer care
And the last of your footprints had faded

l waited for you
After the rains had long gone
And the tears had all but dried up

I was waiting for you
When you found the love in you
When you found yourself

I wait for you
Like dew drops on summer mornings
Waiting for the rain to make them whole again

I'll wait for you
When you've fought the last of your silent battle
When no one else is waiting for you

I'm Art

I'm a poem
Think of me in thoughts
Write me in lines
Express me in stanzas

I'm a song
Hum me as a tune
Sing me as a verse
Play me as a melody

I'm a canvas
Sketch me as an outline
Draw me as a picture
Paint me as colours

I'm the ocean on a day windy
I'm the earth with fire in my belly
I'm a painting with strokes running free
I'm a quill on a writing spree
I'm art
Whichever way you see!

I'm in Your Corner

Whenever emotions weigh you down
And you can see no further
I'm just a heartbeat away
I'm in your corner

When the skies seem dark
And the clouds are a bother
I'll give you my moonlight
I'm in your corner

When you feel the chill
And you can't light a fire
I'll warm you with my words
I'm in your corner

If life seems to be hurrying
And you crave for a breather
I'll coax my time to pause
I'm in your corner

I am Love

"Are you in love?" Somebody asked me
I replied, it's the other way round, love is in me

I am the Storm Chaser

He is mostly calm and composed
The lull before the storm, I think
Little ripples in those ocean eyes
When he tries hard not to blink

Then the storm rises slow
in my heart when he finally blinks
I think he already knows this
How my ship helplessly sinks

A thousand sighs in that instant
When he lovingly holds my sail
An eternity of love in every word
Oh how he makes me blush and pale

The anchor he is to my voyages
Since I found home in his ocean
In my night eyes, he holds his dreams
As we weave tales of such sweet passion

I Be Your Sky

You cannot see me
Only a leap of faith
When you take me in
I'm the air on your breath

I am the fire
If you are cold to your soul
Your desires are mine
I will take you whole

I am the waterfall
Understand my gush first
Endlessly cascade on you
Eternally quench your thirst

If you want a place to rest
I can be the earth
Envelop you in my arms
Cover you in my hearth

And if you want space
I will never deny
You be my moon
I'll be your sky

In Love with My All

Poetess poetess to the world
Beloved lover to one
Writing line after line for all
Feelings conveyed to just one

Face and mind seen by all
Heart and emotions by some
Fully clothed and covered
Soul naked and bare to just one

Spreading smiles everywhere
Only he sees my tears fall
When I come undone before him
And he is in love with my all

In My City

I talked to the sun during the day
Persuaded her to set early today
She obliged saying "That's a pity!"
Oh well, the Moon will be out in my city

The stars were hesitant to shine
After I frowned upon them from cloud (number) nine
A frown steeped in boundless ecstasy
The Moon is a special guest in my city

O what a brilliant dazzling night
My heart shimmering too in the light
My sky has never looked so pretty
The Moon is shining in my city!

In My Head

You came into my life with an unfelt thirst
Unexpected but awaited as the unseasonal rains
I was surprised, taken aback at first
Then I let the feeling sink in..free reigns
(You are mine in my head)

You were a shot of mystery, I got hit
I'm unravelling you now layer by layer
And as I undo you tenderly bit by bit
Ironically, you become my slayer
(I made you mine in my head)

You kill me yet I feel alive
It's your undone love on which I thrive
Deep into your soul as I dive
To get hold of you, I strive
(You are already mine in my head)

My love, don't be sad
It won't kill you, it's not all that bad
I want to belong, not possess
Do to your heart, reassess
(I am yours in my head)

Don't shun, but live the urge
Come with me, feel the surge
Let love and longing merge
(We are one in my head)

In Too Deep

Beauty is skin deep,
Depth has no bottom.
He found her first,
Got lost in her second.

Journey Back Home

The first time those wandering feet stopped at the door
Monsoon was early, the clouds began to pour
Incessant rains and irregular heartbeats became the norm
Doubts were still creeping if this was what they called home

The second time around, the moon was up and about
Monsoon just gone, the wintry sun began to pout
Streaks of golden sunrays warming the still-cloudy abode
Those wandering feet had found their chosen road

Long road home from the clouds and the rain
One step at a time, and those feet walk again
Yet another journey, and back the homing bird flies
At long last, those feet stop where the sun shines!

Just a Heartbeat Away

Only a heartbeat away, I have no use for a bell
All I ever need to do is whisper your name
From the depths of my soul where you now dwell
Please don't vacate; home would never be the same

Kissed by the Wind

Foreword:

I could never explain
And neither could you
How the cracks in our souls
Become the very hinges to latch on to

The other day I ruminated
I spoke to the wind
It was still, I was not

I felt my hair being caressed lightly
at first,
then the storm rose

With such gust
My layers fell off one by one
Until I was naked to my soul

I saw my cracks
I stood watching in disbelief
Asking myself if the storm was me.
The wind spoke then:
"It is time you calmed down"
I smiled, trembling
As the wind kissed me and blew away
With the promise of a gentle breeze

Now every time the wind blows,
I know it is me being exposed
And my layers being unravelled
Like the petals of a flower
Being spread out with each tender stroke

Afterword:

The wind has cracks too
If you are still enough to feel

Layers

When I'm alone with him
My layers I unfold and fold
Leaving behind traces of stories
That no longer remain untold

Lazy Morning Dreams

Lazy morning stirs
With your words
Murmur in lashes

You disperse the rays
Soft kisses
Sunshine in my eyes

Taste of cinnamon
In your breath
I'm grounding the spice

My morning cuppa
Gets me sizzling
Flavoured by your taste

Your fuzzy embrace
Love blanket
Bury myself deep

Your breath on my nape
Summer breeze
You take in my scent

Whisper in my ear
I love yous
Lashes dream away

Leave the Faucet On

The glow on my face you see
Is the love inside of me
Unable to contain, it spills
All over you in spells

I am a faucet in your hand
You turned me on and on around
Now I'm overflowing can you see
Oh don't turn me off, 'I'm finally me'

Let there be Light

When nights are longer than **Days**
and with fading shadows you **Fight**
When moments spent with the one you **Love**
get dimmed by memories of happier **Times**
And from the deep hole of **Emptiness**
You never can seem to **Rise**

When you start doubting the sun*rise*
if indeed there will be sunny *days*
after having spent too long in dark *emptiness*
It becomes your friend, the light you *fight*
Yet you sigh with nostalgia over *times*
that now seem like short-lived *love*

When the one who promised to *love*
whether you falter or you *rise*
gets amnesiac on that vow from *times*
spent in counting those blooming *days*
When every smile becomes a *fight*
Because you have gotten used to the *emptiness*

So much so that this *emptiness*
soothes you in ways your *love*
never could do against your *fight*
Your demons in your head *rise*
strong and dampen your *days*
Sigh! The signs of changing *times*

Hold! Take a cue, from the happy *times*
Maybe there isn't so much *emptiness*
If you embrace the dawn with its promise of sunny *days*
And it's renewed hopes of *love*
Let the sun again, in all its glory, *rise*
And give you a hand in your *fight*

May you get the strength to *fight*
In your dark despair *times*
May you not just stand but *rise*
Far over and above the *emptiness*
To give as many chances to *love*
As you can in your remaining *days*

These eventful *days* spent in peace and *fight*
Rendering *love* the winner all *times*
No more *emptiness* let us all fall and *rise*

Let's Get Lost

You were out of love, I was out of hope
We have never really been able to cope
With the fleeting fickles fireless and the undones
The pretenders, hollows, inanes, and the humdrums

I was 'busying' my time, you were just going on
A twist of fate, the sleepwalking days are gone
Now you found love and I found hope
We no longer sulk, no we don't mope

Untamed I have always been, not of late
Unfettered you are, shackles you hate
Freedom we value, and solitude we cherish
To be running together free and wild is what we wish

Let's break the chains, eyes be mine, dreams you be
Let's be bound, yet be free
Freedom has a price, what's it going to cost
We found each other, now let's get lost

Like the Wind

I often hear you in the whistling of the wind
I catch a glimpse of you in the shadows that fall
I close my eyes and I taste you in my tears
When I open them, I find myself staring at the wall

You've been looking for me everywhere
Peering over footprints on the ground
But if you know where to seek me
You'll find me inside you, not around

Love, many a times, cannot be heard or seen
Miles and miles of space, but the faith cannot be dimmed
If you've been fortunate enough to have been touched by such love
You know it can only be felt like the wind

Lost Forever

I loved you the minute you came
Into my empty arms
And how we grew in love
Bit by bit, our hands became full

And then I was overwhelmed
By the affection you showered
Under shouts cloaked in whispers
And your heated passion for me
In whispers masked by shouts

I do not know anymore
What drew me to you more?
But I do know
The love we felt
And the phases we went through
Were as real and pure as you and me.

You were selfish
You wanted me only for yourself
I'm selfish too
I want myself only for you

You wanted us to know
I wanted them to know

And in this discord
I got lost.
I was found and then I got lost in you
Whereas,
You are lost in me never to be found again.

Love My All

If you love me, you must know me
If you don't know me, you mustn't love me
See, I am love and I am no love
I'm never in between, either below or above

If you know me, you must understand me
If you cannot understand me, you don't know me
See, I am a paradox of the highest order
Also a victim of obsessive disorder

If you understand me, you must not judge me
If you judge me, you never understood me
See, I'm free from prejudices and biases
So I stay away from reservations and judgements

I will give you happiness or I may tear you apart
Whatever I give you, I will give you with all my heart
I will rise in love and in indifference, I may fall
So if you love me, you must love my all!

Love Saga

I'll look into your eyes
And touch your face
I'll say I love you deep
I'll feel your pulse race

I'll smother you with kisses
From your forehead to your toes
Pausing in between to
Let poetry become prose

I'll sit astride you
And hold you so tight
I'll feel your love grow
Let you love me without a fight

Make me your altar
Be my high priest
Worship me all you can
Let all your senses feast

When you are done
I will turn the tables
Let the saga repeat
Let it not be fables

Love Tree

While they
talk about love, the good
and the bad, I'm here witnessing it, writing about it;
experiencing the very essence of it, all that it means,
all that it offers in its wake: the seed
the sprout
shrub
bush
tree
fruit
and the eventual Fall

Love Typos*

My fingers scramble
to write perfect love letters –
scattering typos

Your thoughts in my head
overpowering senses –
fingers can't keep pace!

The sound of your words
touch the fibres of my heart
sending words askew

Try hard as I might
lines go helter skelter with
your name on my lips

The sound of your thoughts
make the tips of my fingers
shake with happiness

Tell me how do I
not lose control when you set
my heart on fire

With these askewed words
forgive me my love typos
Won't you set them straight?

*Written with FT Ledrew

Love Within

Show me your hungry soul
And I'll feed you my vulnerable one
Let us do away with the masks
Let this love be our naked truth

Let us put an end to wars
Waged by our stubborn minds
While the yielding hearts know
Nothing but love that remains

So come to me with nothing on
Save this battered skin of yours
Even then, I will cut through it
I will find and love that what's within

Loving you with all the fire in me

You are house, I'm fire
I am the strings you are the lyre
A symphony being played by a power higher
Reflections of an existential desire

Don't try and sanitize this passion
I am in no need of love lesson
I will love you like it's a crime
You are the love of a lifetime

I want to love you with all my madness
How deep this sense of belongingness
When I think of loving it's only you I see
I want to love you with all the fire in me

Lull and Tide

When he descends
It takes a storm
For her to become calm

Then he kisses her
She becomes still;
Caresses sending ripples though
Underneath her skin

The sky is rapt and
watches in awe
Stars giggle through clouds
Jealous and dark

Unfettered,
they do their divine
intrepid dance

She rises to his call
He retires to her fall
She is the tide
and he, her lull

Make me the Muse of Your Unwritten Poetry

Your undone deeds, unsaid words they never lie
They speak to me through your eyes
Your words of love, whether little or lot
They soothe, in those I find comfort

I've been down and out, you've been laying low
Dreary clouds overhead, moving slow
Let's urge the sky to do away with its bemoans
Ask for some sunlight, we are cold to the bones

Between you and me is a long road
Many moons, many suns, their abode
Seek a way to my soul, find a ruse
Of your unwritten poetry, make me the muse.

Meera and Magdalene: Tales of Devotion

Mary Magdalene was a woman scorned
Labeled a whore but was really a saint
Loving her Lord till death and far beyond
Loved by her Lord more than all else around

Meera, a devotee of her Dark Lord
Krishna as he was known by the world
He had his own consort duly approved
But by Meera, he was so deeply moved

Magdalene followed Jesus everywhere
She loved him with all her heart true and pure
Seven demons cast out of her body faint
When Christ her Lord anointed her a saint

Meera was content with singing praises
In honour of her beloved dark Lord
She travelled alone to lands far and wide
knowing she had her Lord walk by her side

What is common between these two women?
Both knew they had the love of their Lords
And so, although gave themselves to their Lords
They knew that their lords belonged to the world

Midnight Rendezvous

She comes up to the window
He is waiting down by the road
Tonight the moon is out of sight
It's going to be a dark long night

He can see she's been crying
He is weary to the bone
But to put that smile back on her face
He will leave his pain alone

Its midnight the clock tower shows
It's the time when lovers meet
But these are two souls out of love
Listening to their own heartbeat

How's my poetess asks he
She chokes on the word
I'm no poetess says she
"Just a sad woman scorned by her lord"

How beautiful it is to find someone
Who sees the crack and tries
He think she is beautiful
Her brokenness he then beautifies

Her face he says gives him peace
Her words, a lump sweet and sour
Just for her little company, he says
He could go to war

She cries at his words
Clutches her heart, it hurts too soon
"Oh how do I tell you I'm in love
With the shadow of the moon"

He doesn't care who she loves
For her love, he will not put up a fight
"Perhaps someday you will see
I was the brightest star on your moonless night"

Her heart and she are now at war
She hates to break his heart back
He tries to smile his bright smile
But she sees his soul starting to crack.

Morning

This sultry morning
The sun comes up stealthily
Hung on sweaty dreams

Mosaic

You keep losing me
I keep losing you
But we keep finding us

I lose myself in you
You lose yourself in me
We find us in each other

Why, then, should we not be?
It doesn't make sense
To be fragmented
To keep looking away
When you are the mirror
And I'm your kaleidoscope
And together we are a beautiful mosaic

My Scarlet Heart, Your Crimson Veins

Our unfolding love
A honey-glazed dawn
in your orange pekoe sky
My scarlet heart sunset
now flowing freely
through your crimson veins

My mountains heave and sigh
my valley no longer dry
as you infuse me with the freshness
of a dewy lavender
on moon-kissed musky nights

No Bragging about this Love

Hear ye all, will I have a magnificent story to tell
All in good time, of mystery and some good ol' spell
Where fiction doesn't stand a darn chance
Let's just keep doing our divine waltz dance

People come, people go all the time
Onlookers keen or callous, its all fine
Bystanders hankering for some love
When the One is pre-ordained from above

Come and go, come and go as we please
Let's keep them on their toes, let's have some tease
There's no hurry, love's not going anywhere
When the time is right, we will be 'nowhere'

For now, let's just bask in sweet surrender
Sacred virginities, claimed by each other
Sheltered by God and angels in a cove
No, we don't need to brag about this love!

Night and Day

I am the night
that wakes up on you
You are the day
that closes its eyes on me

No Holds Barred

Come as you are, no holds barred
Let me love you with all your scars
I have no use for your cape or mask
Come without facades, that's all I ask

Step out of the shadow, come out in the light
Let me be your reflection, I promise you a beautiful sight
Don't dwell in the past, nothing does ever last
This nakedness you feel, this too shall past

I'll be your light, I see your dark
Underneath your body naked stark
Those knots you so conceal
Let them show, let them reveal

With care shall I untie those
Until you are then finally free
from the inflictions of your mind
As free as an untamed heart can be

You will fall in love this time
Deeper than you have ever been
With the person that you truly are
Beautiful broken soul only I have seen

Nothing Like Love

There's nothing like the comfort of a warm bed on a cold
wintry night
Except maybe those loving arms
Which are still holding you when you suddenly wake up
in the middle of the night.

There's nothing like waking up to soft golden rays
streaming in through the drapes
Except maybe that sweet tender kiss
That makes you smile dreamily through half open eyes

There's nothing like getting back home after a hard day
And feeling your senses relax on your favourite couch
Except maybe that eager embrace that assures you your
absence was felt

There's nothing like peels of laughter
Over an anecdote shared among friends
Except maybe that one sly smile
From the one who knows the story behind the joke

There's nothing like the sound of soft music
To lull you to peaceful slumber
Except maybe the pitter-patter of rains on a tin roof
Murmurs being drowned while shadows dance on the wall

There's nothing like being in the wild
Finding your way in Neverland
Except maybe getting lost in the wilderness of dreams
with the one who dreams with you

There's nothing like rapt attention by poets galore to your
lines
Recognition of an effort well done
Except maybe those two familiar eyes that are taking in
each word without blinking
A knowing smile in those eyes that lights up yours

Now and Forever

When I said I love you
I did not know how much.
How could I measure something that keeps flowing
endlessly?
I still don't know how much I love you
I can't tell you
I just know when I think of love
You are the only one that comes to my head

When I think of my life gone by
I wonder where were you
When we could have been.
When I think of the future
I see only you
Sitting by the fireplace
while I read to you your favourite poem
And you look at me with such tenderness you cannot
explain either

I do not know how much I love you
I just know I look at you the way I look at no one else
And I know I have started looking like you
I'm told I'm becoming you

So, my beloved forgive me
For I really cannot tell you how much I love you
But I can tell you this
I want you now and forever

Offering

Look!
The seed of love you planted
In my barren heart
Has bloomed into a garden

Blossoms of all shades grow now
Vibrant oranges, flamboyant reds, sunny yellows, subtle
blues

And here my love
I offer you
from my blooming heart

The most beautiful flower
In all colours and in no colour

On Waking

I
am
awake
but I feel
so lost in my dreams
of yesterday and tomorrow
I cannot tell If I am living in my today
I am asleep, floating with you in a cloudless dream
I think I am afraid to wake,
To open my eyes
lest I see
you are
but
gone

So
let
me dream
on, my love.
Please don't wake me up
and, if you must, please
let me find-
always-
you,
here

Paint your Heart

Shake your head all you can
I am yet to seal my love for you
The moment I kiss you entirely for once
You'll know I never lied

The day I trace my name
On the canvas of your back
My fingertips will quiver no more
For they will have found their perch

Then I shall dip those in my heart
Take out colours of your choice
Red, orange, yellow, blue, I got it all
Lovingly, I shall paint your heart

Perpetual Night

I have a perpetual night inside
of me but not the dark desolate kind
A selenophile would know what I mean
A beautiful moonlit night every night

I chatted with the moon the other night
I asked "why don't you come every night?"
I'm wary of my blemishes being seen
So said the moon with sadness and some fright

I clutched my chest, no longer could I hide
the pain I felt inside, you know I tried
I let the soft silvery moonlight flow
through my eyes, oh how we both sat and cried

I set the Moon, from inhibitions, free
I am now the night, the moon dwells in me!

Petals and Ferns

A drop of sunshine
A pinch of rain
I'm good to go with you
In my dreams again

Shine on me, my love
Pour on me some more
Show me your pulsating heart
Love me to my throbbing core

Make love to me on a bed
Of roses with all the thorns
A reminder of all my flaws
Lovely petals and plain ferns

And I will love you
With all my heart and mind
Wherever you go or I
A way to be with you, I'll find

*Phases**

A Crescent flickered
When you first knocked on my door
Half-covered shy smiles

My clear, starlit eyes
Twinkled in sweet reflection
Bathed by your beauty

Gibbous then it got
Mysterious layers now
Unearthing with care

Excavating smiles
And tender whispers of love
From my swooning soul

No waxing this moon
Only hearts melting with warmth
In solar phases

Head bowed like Earth's tilt
I spilled into the craters
Of your summer eyes

I won't let it wane
Sweet nothings won't go sour with
My heart in your veins

As orbital love
locks me in its deep embrace
with gravity's kiss

*Written with FT Ledrew

Poetry Everywhere

Close them shallow eyes on your face
And open those of your mind divine
Come out of the shadow of reluctance
Come forth, with all your glories shine!

I am not afraid, one day I will cease to be
I only have fears, some day my ink will pale
When I die, I will become one with the wind
But for as long as I live, poetry I shall exhale!
- Nandita 'Manan' Yata

Poetry is love and love is poetry
In between you see the beauty
All the manifestations in all its glory
No matter the language – wordless or flowery

There's a line in every word, a verse in every line
A story hidden to be unwrapped in its layer
So open the eyes of the mind divine
When you do, you'll see there's poetry everywhere

Poetry Loves me too

A poet is really a vagabond
Caught in a tangle of words momentary
The tongue can never become the heart
Unless we find our poetry

I have a fountain pen in my bosom
The nib keeps piercing all through the day
When night falls, the ink flows on its own
And then my heart bleeds the yearning away

I write because I can see the light
Even when dark clouds overcast the sky
My flightless bird finds the strength
To steer her way through words that never lie

I write because I love poetry
An ocean of emotions within me stir
I write because poetry loves me too
That's the only thing worth living for

Poetry Rains

My words you breathe in
Your syllables I inhale
We then exhale deep
Glorious droplets of rain
Poetry drenching us insane

Rain on Me

Don't let love be a trickle
Come pour on me
I've waited, parched
as neglected soil can be

I gave away my umbrella
I never had one anyway
Let me now get drenched
in your love in every way

Reading Braille

As the world turns
So do I…
I am not shy
Of giving love
There, what you see
Is what I am!

If you see me look at you with love in my eyes
It's because I'm letting you read me with all your senses
ensnared.
And if you see me closing my eyes on you
It's because I am learning to read you like a blind one
would read braille!

Real Men Cry

His earliest memories were "boys don't cry"
Timid little thing he was, trouble getting by
When the black dog bit him, he stopped the tears
He conditioned himself to never show his fears

Grew up in the shadow of toughness of a man
He was the boy that happened without a plan
Angry little boy, aloof he spent his childhood
Not too popular among kids in the neighbourhood

Sulking always, couldn't figure out why
Consoled himself by saying I'm shy
Petrified by his own secrets, no dispute there
His deep heart, could never imagine, to bare

He looked all around for something
Didn't really know what he was missing
Fell in love with a girl, he couldn't tell
Every night under covers, he would yell

With no one to hear his silent cries
He succumbed to different kind of highs
Hoped for a new day, the brightest of skies
Was so frustrated by his own lies

Gave love a chance again as he got older
Decided to overcome, his invisible boulder
The woman he met, saw in her a saviour
His soul rescued, he felt so much braver

Overwhelmed by her love, he began to open up
Shared with her what all these years, he had bottled up
He felt relieved, freedom from the shackles of his mind
And the black dog came haunting to remind

All his fears came flooding back to him
Those memories of fighting back with fake vim
A sense of peace engulfed him, no longer superficially
high
Letting the tears flow on her bosom, as she said "real
men cry"

Rustler in the Woods

Woke up from my sleep
Was lost in the wilderness
Of my fallen dreams
These woods they beckon me now
And I walk bare feet

My soles are tickled
The rustling of fallen leaves
Senses awoken
I hear you sweet whistling wind
Music, when sweet voices fall

Sanctity

Ask the world not to call me anymore
For, I am so lost in an endless stream
I am caught up in a tangle of words
I am beckoned by a novella dream

Ask the world to go look somewhere else
I have been found by my universe
This is where I have always belonged
This is what has always belonged to me

Tell the world there is no need to worry
I am guided by the eternal light
That flickers in some far faraway land
Travels all the way and glows in my heart

Tell the world I have never been better
I am pure, all my sins have now been washed
These are our sacred grounds that we tread on
Deeper than what we could ever fathom

Sapphire, Black Diamond

The departing sun played tricks on me
As he shifted his gaze towards my eastern skies
The deep blue ocean that was once in me
I found it sparkling in those sapphire eyes

His explorer eyes eager to seek and please
Peered back and forth towards my sight
My dark eyes meanwhile perched behind the glass
Suddenly glowed black like midnight

Blue locked in black, unblinking moments
In each, a hundred stories abound
They should make a movie out of it
Call it Sapphire and Black Diamond

Scarlet

It's the dusk for some
Or maybe the break of dawn
The colours you paint
Brilliant blues and fresh greens
It's always Scarlet for me

Seasons of Love

May was when the sun began to glitter
In a dark, dingy and cloudy place
Every passing day, hope started to glimmer
Gray gloomy clouds fading without a trace

Then came June heralding new promises
Of never-been better days
As two lonely hearts met with nervousness
Having enacted their pretences and plays

July was still fresh in their memories
As they grinned from ear to ear
They went back their own ways for now
Promising to be together in the future near

With the falling leaves and changing colours
August ushered in a season of loneliness
The two hearts getting fonder and sadder
Yearning for this newfound closeness

September rains did nothing to help
The two separated, not by choice
While one held on to dear poetry
The other sought solace in her voice

Countdown began with the start of October
Their ecstasy knew no bounds
The separation that seemed forever

Their feet were now leaving the grounds

Alas! Winter came too soon for the sun-kissed hearts
November got spent in hello and so long
Time goes by so quickly when you don't have it
Wishing you could stop the ticking along

Cold grew heavy with the onset of December
Hearts heavy with snow that fell nowhere else
Loneliness diseased and crippled their senses
Hope dragged along like a leper wretch

Scoundrel snow started thawing with tepid warmth
When January brought some respite
The two reunited after what seemed like ages
And even the cold now seemed alright

But February came just too soon
And brought with it a forked road
The two went separate ways preordained
Cheeks stained as hot tears rolled

A lot of uncertainty came with the Ides of March
Unseasonal snow, dark clouds and torrential rain
No sight of April in the horizon
Wondering if May will come again

Shaken

When I'm with you,
I become love
When you write for me,
I become your poetry

And I would go to the end of the world to be with you,
If fate wills it.
And I would try and defy fate,
should it not will so.
But I would die
knowing I gave all I could
to be with the one
who shook my soul

Shine on, Love

Though you are the light to my dark
You have a darkness of your own
I have seen your soul naked stark
Upon mine, your darkness shone

I have seen you laugh with the world
I have seen those tears fall with me
For me, you have come undone my love
With you, I have become truly me

Poets with obligatory paper swords
We are partners in love, dark and light
We found us starless behind our starry words
We found love on a breezy moon-deserted night

Shout it Out

You're now every love poem I've read about
You are the one who my poems are about
Oh please don't ask me to suppress this bout
Only I know what it takes not to shout

There is peace and calm in the blinding light
Then there is wildness in the serene night
I am caught in between and I am both
Let me shout it out, let me bring it forth

It was getting too noisy, just too loud
When you made the world silent all around
And that is why I fell in love with you
That is how you fell in love with me too

So come my dear, come now, let's do this right
Let us not just be whispers of the night!

Simile and Metaphor

Love can happen anytime and anywhere
Between anyone
Yes, even a simile and a metaphor!

All it takes is a tiny spark.
That little connect at the right place
Not geographical though,
rather mental, emotional and spatial.

And when it does happen
With winds blowing in the right direction
There is every chance that this tiny spark
Will turn into something so massive, so powerful
Like a wildfire
That will burn everything on its way
The simile, the metaphor…
Until no euphemism remains
And only love in all its true dysphemic glory will shine
through.

Smouldering Ember

He fell in love with her when
She pointed to the sun on a cloudy day
She showed him green red and yellow
When his gaze was only dismal gray

Everyday, she makes him fall in love
Deeper than he has ever been
She gets him dreaming like never before
She's the loveliest dream he's ever seen

He cried when she showed him how to love
The hard shell all reduced to dust
He hungers for her one more touch
He finds himself torn between love and lust

He's played with fire many times
Never before had he burned this way
The smouldering ember that he's become
Now in her fire, he wants to burn away

Someone

Find someone who is not afraid to fall in love
Even with your dark side
Someone who is crazy about you
and has no problems admitting it
Someone who thinks you are the reason
he/she knows love
Someone who wants to be consumed
by your love

Someone who believes in soulmates
Understands the term twin flame
Keeps trying to win you over
Who wants to rise every time there is a fall
Someone who believes love is a verb
Says I love you every time you cry
Who doesn't hold your weaknesses against you

Be with someone who accepts gifts well
Who knows your worth
Who appreciates you every day
Makes you feel indispensable

Fall in love with someone who makes you feel
like you are his/her first and last love
Who goes that extra mile
just to make you smile
Someone who thinks there's no such thing
as too much love

Someone who feels blessed
to be in love with you
Someone kind

But, before you find that someone,
be that someone.

Soul Reprise

He comes home late, she is waiting
There is resolve in his voice
He can see she has been crying
Indulge her tonight, he makes his choice

She isn't sulking or an emotional mess
Guilty he pleads, for not showing enough
He tries to tell her all about his stress
But she already knows his day was rough

She can see the fatigue in his eyes
Just as he can make out the anticipation in hers
Both fight their own feuds during the day
But their love, at the end of the day, never suffers

She sits him down beside her
Looks at him with eyes full of yearning
He pulls her closer to his chest
Oh what a beautiful familiar feeling!

They lie in silence, eyes wide shut
Letting their hearts do the talking
As he plays with one strand of her hair
And she basks in such sweet loving

Their heartbeats quicken, their love gets fierce
Some soul guy in the background gets singing
The lights are dimmed, the heads are rested
The shadows on the wall are now dancing

The music stops, the dancing comes to a halt
Beads of sweat shimmer on the skin
She turns away, his lips on her nape
Second time, soul reprise ready to begin

Spring Always

Could the cosmos be in eternal love
with me, for it keeps guiding me to
some place where the water never
dries, where it's eternal spring!
The chill of winter leaves
brazen hearts frozen
but hope survives
because then
comes the
Spring!
The
Cosmos
does indeed
seem to love me
endlessly, while you
become the harsh winter
Chilling the Fall on its way
Freezing this love right to my core
The warmth of your summer memories
spreads as wildfire from my every pore

Spring is Here!

The bees are buzzing
The birds are humming
Sweet tunes of love
Spring is here!

My fingers are strumming
Your heart goes drumming
To the rhythm of mine
Spring is here!

I sing songs of joy
You go mad oh boy
With renewed ecstasy
Spring is here!

My cheeks are flushed
My mouth is shushed
Silence makes sound
Spring is here!

I dance away the dark
You watch awestruck
Moon blushes red
Spring is here!

Cold winter departs
Thawing frozen hearts
Perfect harmony
Spring is here!

Goodbye frost
Anticipated warmth
Hello interim lush
Spring is here!

Starry Eyes

Started on a journey with my hands empty
Was looking for myself but I stumbled upon him
Fate works in mysterious ways and I found my calling
My life has a meaning, now that my cup is filled to the
brim

All it takes is faith and prayers get answered
Believe and wishes do come true
Life is a happy riot of colours for the dreamer
Not just dismal gray or melancholic blue

I kept on believing never stopped dreaming
Till my dreams found a place in your eyes
Now your eyes are starry like never before
Little priceless jewels adorning my skies

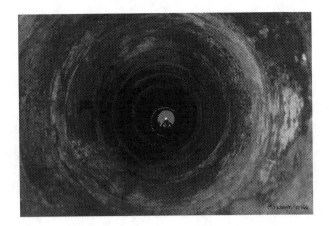

The Abyss

I'm so trapped
in this unending abyss
Forever falling
No respite.

And if I were to die
In this fall
I'd be happy.
Knowing that
I lived the fullest
That I could ever have
Then when I was trying to rise.

The Artist Answers The Muse*

If
you were
an artist,
what would I be?
A subject of love
or an object of lust?
Would you paint and display me,
hang me as a priceless Van Gogh
or forget me as a worthless scrap?
Your masterpiece or neglected showpiece?
A masterpiece painted of divine love,
I would hang on the wall of my heart;
sit your bust on my soul's mantle;
stand your statue in a shrine,
for all the world to see,
beauty on display.
if I was an
artist and
you, my
muse.
*Written with FT Ledrew

The Fatal Fight

The sun has long set
But the journey goes on
Your wait keeps me restless
Now tell me who's lovelorn

I have waited for you
Countless days and nights
Had soliloquies with the Moon
Where I told him about the sun

The Moon was terribly livid
That the Sun shone even at night
I said the sun never sets on me
The Moon and I had a fatal fight

The silvery light trickled one last time
I caught it, it fell from my eyes
The Ocean that I used to be
Swallowed the tears, freed us from the lies

The Ocean died, dried up by the sun
Out rose the water nymph at noon
The sun caressed her with his loving warmth
She no longer howls at the Moon

The Highwayman

He is like the wind
Never at one place
Sometimes a cool breeze on a hot sweltering day
Other times a hurricane that uproots everything on its
way

An untethered stallion to the world
He is the highwayman on the run
But for the one who knows and waits
He is the homeward-bound man

Someone who went high and low
Hoping to build a house of his own
His illusion shattered a hundred pieces
When he realized she was his home

To be or not to be was a question unsettling
Resisting the change was quite a daunting task
If you ask me, he's put away his cloak
For the one who saw right through his mask

The Island

Oh sailor, let me sail along with you
Take us to an island far away
Let this be the last ferry of our lives
Let us cast the past away

We have sailed enough stormy waters
We have both had our share
We are tired of our wanderings
Now let us just put flowers on my hair

You can call me a dreamer
My feet have broken free
The horizon is just around the corner
And the island is where I want to be

The One

When I first saw you
I could never see myself
Through broken fragments
Of the mirror that you were
You said you were damaged

I didn't want to know
Who ripped the soul out of you
I fought my way in
I just knew it had to be
Me to piece you whole again

You did not believe
When I told you I loved you
That my soul loved yours
Now you know what it is like
To be made love to your soul

I got bruised and hurt
Your sharp edges cut through mine
And I smoothened those
I glued them back with my cracks
A perfect mosaic it made

Now I look at you
I cannot see you at all
You have become me
Just like I have become you
When you look into my eyes

The Pearl

Down in the ocean
Slept a pearl
Up on the surface
I was trying to swirl

Along came my boatman
Who rocked the waters
I asked him to stop
He gave me the shivers

He stretched out his hand
I clutched his arm
I pulled him hard
Such was his charm

Both fell down
Thud and wet
In search of the pearl
On a journey we set

Dolphins and sea urchins
Greeted us on the way
We waved and dived
Deeper and further away

The glitter of the pearl
Now we could see
In the quest of life
As hurried as we could be

The oyster played games
Open and shut
Undaunted we stood
Patience doesn't hurt

The pearl in our hands
Shiny and dreamy
The pearl in our hearts
Glowing eternally

The Riverbed

He is an invisible riverbed
Over which she lovingly flows
His surface is what others see
His depth only she knows

She was an oasis of love
For the aimless wanderer that he was
Someone kind smiled on him from above
He stopped running, she's where he chose to pause

She nourished the life in him
How he was parched to the core
She watered and nurtured him
There's nothing he could ask for more

His thirst is quenched, he is calm
Her waters never fail to caress him
He is bathed in love, wrapped in warmth
Now he is her and she is him

Till Death Do Us Apart

In the solemn spaces between sunsets and sunrises, we find sublime hope.
We borrow the moonlight to fall in love.
In this saga of preludes and postludes, we find fragments of our hearts strewn along the sacred interludes.

And I promise you, that I will continue to hold your hand and walk with you even on the darkest of nights where we may find nothing for miles and miles ahead. Only the solace of our fingers intertwined in between each other's interludes.

Wherever we go or wander, my heart will pick up those pieces of your heart that you so lovingly scattered for me to find my way back into yours. This is how we will always help each other find ourselves together where we belong.
Till death do us apart!

Under the Old Oak Tree

There was no moon
that night yet I shone
my brightest
When you romanced me
under the old oak tree

Your hand on my heart
Thumping out loud
"Is that for me?" you had asked
My eyes downcast, looking up slow
That had said it all

You moved in closer
Your lips nearing mine
Your heart now pounding
As I slipped in my hand inside
And I felt you swell

Both hearts now beating love
"Yes that's you and I"
passion and desires converging
Stars giggled and hid
It was a black night

There was no moon
That night yet we dazzled
The sky
When I romanced you
under that old oak tree

Warehouse of Love

You all are in love with me
Oh yes, I'm a heartbreaker
You'd see I have so much love in me
If only you were to delve deeper

I give my love to all everywhere
I keep collecting hearts you see
I have a trophy house within
And you are all under my skin

Oh please don't misread my words
Everyone gets a piece of me
It's never too crowded where I love
I'm a warehouse of love as can be

But who am I in love with?
That's a mystery I won't solve
Just love, and be loved by me
Love needs no answer nor resolve

When We Held Hands

I held your hand today
Unbreakable vow made in silence
While our scars bore witness

You showed me your callouses
And I, my bruises
That moment of unknown intimacy

Your eyes spoke of the pain
But your heart overflowed with desire
When you tightened your grasp

Even in your brokenness
You looked perfect
You surrendered whole,
our hands clasped tight

Neither one of us spoke
Suddenly your eyes shone with new light
And my face glowed in your reflection

I looked and I smiled
I saw and you smiled

We were home...

When You Looked into My Eyes

The first time you looked
into my eyes, I knew
you'd start living there.
That every morning,
you'd have to peel
me from your dreams.

The first time I looked at you,
the azure skies
reflected brilliantly in
your sapphire eyes.
And the subtle hint
of difference between
the two shades
became the glimmer in my dark eyes.

And I saw
my sky,
my ocean,
my world,
just like you saw
your mysterious universe
in mine,
waiting to be unravelled
with every blink.

I knew, the first time you looked into my eyes,
you'd start living there.

Wrapped

1000 words of love
Wrapped up in five syllables
"When I see you smile"

You Made a Poet Out of Me

The silence of the lonely night
Cuts deep through empty spaces
The whispers of the anxious heart
Fade slow into loud silences

You lie there, I lie here
Words said and unsaid in between
Sleep eludes, sleep deceives
Tired eyes with dreams seen and unseen

The cruel winter did nothing to freeze
I saw my feet had broken free
I became the lushest of springs
I was no longer a dead tree

I was searching for an answer
Asking myself to be or not to be
Struggling with words that refused to form
And then you made a poet out of me

Your Name

The sky paled as I
drew a constellation of
your name in my heart

Your Spell

You
The one
To make me
Fall deeper than
Love

You
The one
Spreading out
The rhymes in my
Thought

I
See you
Look at me
With tenderness
Such

I
Feel you
All around
When I close my
Eyes

Eyes
Aglow
With your light
Warm within my
Heart

And
When I
Open them
It's again just
You

Hear
My words
I love you
I do confess
So

Yes
I am
An addict
For your love and
You

I am not afraid, one day I will cease to be
I only have fears, some day my ink will pale
When I die, I will become one with the wind
But for as long as I live, poetry I shall exhale!
                                    - Nandita 'Manan' Yata

About the Author

A PhD in Japanese Studies from Jawaharlal Nehru University, New Delhi, and proficient in six languages, Nandita 'Manan' Yata's first love is poetry. She has been writing in earnest for a little over a year. She is an erudite scholar; her writings chronicle her deep observations of life and love. A prolific writer with a universal voice, her poems (including Haiku, Senryu, Tanka and Sonnet) are a blend of personal experience and literary experimentation. She lives in New Delhi.

Passion in Poetry: Whispers from the Soul is Nandita's debut book of poetry. She takes you on a journey into the beautifully bare soul, the intricacies of the mind and the infinite space for love in the heart. Besides poetry, she loves to indulge in music and dance. She confesses she is in love with artists in general and poets in particular. Her favorite poets are Pablo Neruda and Rumi, often drawing inspiration from them. She is a spiritual person and is an ardent believer that there is no such thing as too much love. She also says, she holds the universe within her believing it to be a manifestation of cosmic love. She holds a deep love for humanity and her love for people and her sensitivity to the world around her often manifest themselves in her writings. She loves her solitude though and says it's her sacred space where she frequently engages in deep conversations with the universe.

Printed in the United States
By Bookmasters